Endor

M000280378

Many of you are having the biggest spiritual battle of your life. This teaching will get you through to the *biggest* door of God's favor and glory in history!

SID ROTH
Host, *It's Supernatural!*

Credible. Biblical. Gifted. Authentic. Humble. These are words that describe the teachings and ministry of Ana Werner. In your hand you have an equipping resource with an edge of cutting truth combining spiritual-warfare understanding with revelatory insight for our times. It is my honor to endorse the ministry of our seer teacher, Ana Werner.

James W. Goll
God Encounters Ministries
GOLL Ideation LLC

As an executive TV producer, I first met Ana Werner when she appeared on our television program, *It's Supernatural!* with host Sid Roth.

I immediately recognized her gifting as a seer and a fire-starter! Then, on the Sid Roth tour in Israel, again I was able to receive ministry from her firsthand as the glory of God was emanating through her.

In her brand-new book, *The Warrior's Dance*, she shares about the vision she had of an end-time war between the enemy and his army and the Bride of Messiah. God has imparted to her how to be victorious over the forces of darkness, even in the midst of the battle!

And the good news is that you don't need to be a seer or a prophet to use these God-given tactics!

This is a revelatory book that will help prepare you to be a part of a company of believers who will wage victorious spiritual warfare through communion with Holy Spirit and synchronicity with the heavenly realm.

This is a must-read book for any believer, in light of the powerful battle between God and the forces of evil that is now manifesting in this broken world. A world sorely needing Jesus!

WARREN MARCUS
Executive TV Producer of Sid Roth's *It's Supernatural!*

May I say, "What person does not have questions about disappointments, offenses, grief, and loss? What person has problems not understanding the way God moves in our lives during these times? And is there a way to have an unoffended heart so that we can receive everything that God has for us?" All these questions are so beautifully answered in this exciting new book by Ann Werner, *The Warrior's Dance*. The title itself will give you a God idea on how to combat the enemy and see victory in every area these questions cover. Her personal stories and examples of dancing in the Spirit will open up new ways to fight the devil and win! This revelation about how the kingdom works will give you insight into being a victor instead of a victim!

PATSY ROSALES
Executive Assistant to Dr. Marilyn Hickey
MHM—Executive Services/Global

I love to read books that carry the heart of God. These books come from a personal encounter and revelation from the Lord Himself. There are times that works masquerade as being from this dimension but are really just originating from the souls of men. In *The Warrior's Dance*, however, Ana Werner unveils that heart and passion of the Father over us as His children. Read this book with not just an open mind but an open spirit. I believe it will propel you to a new place of encounter with Jesus Himself.

ROBERT HENDERSON
Bestselling author of *The Courts of Heaven* series

In Ana Werner's new book, *The Warrior's Dance*, she beautifully unfolds what it means to have the heart of a warrior in the midst of spiritual warfare. As Christians, we are to carry His power, love, and authority into all the world, but it's difficult to do that when we haven't learned the dance of a warrior. This book will not only challenge you to properly engage in the fight, but to win the battle and enjoy the blessings that God has for your life!

RYAN BRUSS
Author of *Carrying the Presence*
www.reviveus.org

Ana Werner has masterfully intertwined her own stories, scriptures, and principles of dealing with offense. All kinds of offenses! I was fascinated with the variety of situations with which she has dealt. It's an excellent book, very solid as well as providing strategies for facing offenses. I love the way she talks about the dance. Every challenge, every strategy can be considered a type of dance. To dance is to worship and worship routs the enemy. She is transparent, and in that transparency she is victorious—constantly seeing that God has something better that overcomes every situation or offense. I love this book; it is so refreshing. Just go ahead and get this book; it will change you.

BARBARA J. YODER
Lead Apostle, Shekinah Regional Apostolic Center
Breakthrough Apostolic Ministries Network
www.shekinahchurch.org

It is our pleasure to endorse Ana's latest book, *The Warrior's Dance*. Clothed with humility, power, and the love of God, Ana goes forward with Jesus at her side. She hears and sees Him well, and she is quick to obey. We know of the enemy's frequent attacks on Ana and her family and of the conflicts she enters because of these attacks. Ana and her family are real people with real life issues, and she offers real solutions and guidance for us to follow. Some of the warfare she has faced will surprise you; it did us. As a senior Christian leader once said, "Christians are born on a battlefield." This book will assist you in securing the victory that Christ has already won for you on that battlefield.

DORIS and LEE HARMS
Directors, Heartland Healing Rooms

In these last days God is releasing great wisdom from heaven to empower the body of Christ. Ana Werner's book is a one such joyous work, full of golden nuggets of revelation and eye-opening experiences that will change your life and ministry forever.

Soak in it and allow God to renew your strength and He will also grant you a new vision for your life.

JOAN HUNTER
Author/Evangelist
TV host of *Miracles Happen!*

In Ana's new book, she has been given a series of revelations that will give you keys of wisdom and knowledge that shall help you be more than an overcomer, by the grace of Jesus! These insights, given by the Father through the Spirit of Jesus, will give you a divine advantage over your adversary so that you can be victorious in every area of life!

PASTOR TONY KEMP
President of the Acts Group
Vice President of Messianic Vision

The Warrior's Dance by Ana Werner powerfully outlines the steps all believers need to take to keep moving forward in God. For those who struggle, it will help you change position from past failure into present victory and a fruitful future. For those who already have a steady spiritual rhythm, it will encourage you in your daily intimacy with the Lord as your read down-to-earth testimonies and receive heavenly insights.

The Warrior's Dance is an inspirational, prophetic revelation of how to overcome our enemy. Ana Werner has combined spiritual truths with visions from heaven! Heavenly keys to victory! The Lord gave Ana dancing warrior shoes which gave her breakthrough in her time of warfare. Those shoes are available to you! It's time to dance. This is your time to overcome! This is your time of victory!

WARD SIMPSON
President, GOD TV

Warriors for the Lord experience spiritual battles and there are many books written on that subject. But Ana Werner's book, *The Warrior's Dance*, brings a uniquely different perspective of a dancing warrior and battling from a place of rest, both of which are intriguing paradoxes!

Ana's book is full of revelation, wisdom, and keys to walk in victory as she shares her personal battles and life lessons she has gained from supernatural encounters with the Holy Spirit. Her willingness to be honest and vulnerable is an on-ramp for the Holy Spirit to bring profound transformation through her stories.

This is not a book you can read quickly if you are willing to engage in her probing questions that expose hooks and landing strips of the enemy. Ana ministers to you prophetically as well as encouraging you to pray life-altering prayers for freedom! She helps you to find Jesus *in* your battles and gives you hope from heaven's perspective!

LINDA VALEN
Ministry Director, Master Potter, Inc.
info@masterpotter.com
www.jillaustinlegacy.com

Ana's book will have you dancing for joy upon what once held you back and/or tried to shut you down. As you read you will see in your hand the keys to victory over the plot of the enemy—reclaiming what has been stolen as you dance upon injustice, eyes locked with Jesus. This book will bring a shift to how you view warfare as your confidence in the Lord soars to new heights. Jesus has set you free to dance the warrior's dance as His beloved bride and the teachings and revelation in this book are the springboard you've been waiting for!

KRISSY NELSON
Author, TV Host, Founder
Created for the Impossible

My friend Ana Werner in her new book, *The Warrior's Dance,* will teach you how use the Word of God and worship as a mighty weapon against the enemy. We need to go deeper into these areas in these last days as we see the great harvest come in with signs and wonders following.

DR. KEVIN L. ZADAI
Founder and President of Warrior Notes
School of Ministry
kevinzadai.com

Some people you meet and instantly know they are a friend of God and have made His presence their perpetual home. Ana Werner is such a person. Her childlike joy imparts wide-eyed wonder as she talks of encounters with God. *The Warrior's Dance* imparts this same awe and wonder and yet equally releases practical wisdom and a spiritual road map to deeper heart connection. In these pages you will discover keys to thriving, even in times of spiritual warfare, and sustain a flourishing heart. It is our joy to recommend this book to you, but even more, to commend our friend Ana to you as a true lover of God's presence and one who has touched His glory realm.

BEN and JODIE HUGHES
Pour It Out Ministries
Author, *When God Breaks In*
www.pouritout.org

There are moments when you come across books that give you line upon line of information, but then there are books that take you on a revelatory journey into understanding. My dear friend Ana has captured the heartbeat of heaven in her amazing new book, *The Warrior's Dance*. Talk about powerful nuggets and real-life accounts packed within every page from front to back; you won't want to put this book down. Ana has been marked by God not only for this hour but for generations to come. This book not only trumpets the voice of the Lord but creates a realm of visibility and tangibility for all who read it to see and step into the various dimensions of God. Get ready to shift from glory to glory as a victorious warrior!

TORREY MARCEL HARPER
Director, Global Prayer Room, NYC
Leader Pastor, Habitation Church

It is our kingdom inheritance to walk in His light, freedom, and victory. However, there are many believers who do not know how to maneuver through spiritual warfare in a victorious warrior dance and stance. The truth is, we don't fight for victory but from victory. A victory already won by Jesus. We must learn and activate the wisdom and warrior's dance to walk out and appropriate what He has won for each of us. Ana has done an exceptional job laying out the truth of how to shift from a stance of defeat to engaging a position of victory. It is a now word and a vital message. Be encouraged and strengthened to walk out your victory in partnership with Jesus, our King who reigns above every demon and all darkness. Thank you, Ana, for this timely and necessary word! *The Warrior's Dance* is a must-read for every believer.

REBECCA GREENWOOD
Christian Harvest International
Strategic Payer Apostolic Network
Author of *Authority to Tread, Let Our Children Go, Defeating Strongholds of the Mind, Glory Warfare*

Ana Werner's latest book, *The Warrior's Dance,* is a divine toolbox for this new era. Full of tools, revelation, heavenly insight, and keys to bring you further into your destiny, walk in greater freedom in Christ, and deeper in encounter with Jesus. This book carries an impartation for you to see like you have never seen before and to walk in all He has for you. This book will activate and help prepare you for all God has for you. It's a banqueting table of glorious truth and revelation. I highly recommend this glorious book to you and my beautiful friend Ana Werner.

LANA VAWSER
Founder of Lana Vawser Ministries
Author of *The Prophetic Voice of God*

God uniquely appoints some to be prophets (in the case with Ana Werner, a seer-prophet), *not* to hear from Heaven for you, but rather, to help you recognize, discern and yes, see what is going on in the spirit realm more clearly. Why? So you can always be walking in sync and in step with the move of the Spirit. This is the rhythm of victorious spiritual warfare—this is truly *The Warrior's Dance.*

We need spiritual warfare books now more than ever, as it's a topic that is becoming lost on this next generation. But let me insert one caveat there: I am looking for warfare books that position the people of God to fight from the place of victory, instead of being hyper-focused on the devil, demons and darkness. Yes, we need to be acutely aware of these forces, but not for the sake of being preoccupied with the next step the devil is making; but rather, Ana shows us how to walk in step with the next move of the Holy Spirit that you can position and align yourself with Heaven's dance of victory.

It's my joy to enthusiastically recommend this amazing book and this author. She writes not as a spiritual warfare theologist or theorist, but as one who truly practices what she preaches!

LARRY SPARKS
LarrySparksMinistries.com
Publisher, Destiny Image
Author of *Breakthrough Faith* and
co-author of *Accessing the Greater Glory*

the
warrior's
dance

DESTINY IMAGE BOOKS BY ANA WERNER

The Seer's Path

Seeing Behind the Veil

Accessing the Greater Glory (with Larry Sparks)

the
warrior's
dance

A Seer's Guide
to Victorious
Spiritual Warfare

Ana Werner

Dedication

I dedicate this book to my mother, Marie. You are one of
the strongest women I know. You have persevered through
much opposition most of your life. Your walk with the Lord
and your stance to remain faithful in His goodness is incredible! You and Dad are both warriors from what you have
walked through!

© Copyright 2020–Ana Werner

All rights reserved. This book is protected by the copyright laws of the United States of America. This book may not be copied or reprinted for commercial gain or profit. The use of short quotations or occasional page copying for personal or group study is permitted and encouraged. Permission will be granted upon request. Unless otherwise identified, Scripture quotations are taken from the NEW AMERICAN STANDARD BIBLE®, Copyright © 1960, 1962, 1963, 1968, 1971, 1972, 1973, 1975, 1977, 1995 by The Lockman Foundation. Used by permission. Scripture quotations marked NIV are taken from the HOLY BIBLE, NEW INTERNATIONAL VERSION®, Copyright © 1973, 1978, 1984, 2011 International Bible Society. Used by permission of Zondervan. All rights reserved. Scripture quotations marked TPT are taken from *The Passion Translation*, Copyright © 2014, 2015, 2016, 2017, www.thepassiontranslation. com. Used by permission of BroadStreet Publishing Group, LLC, Racine, Wisconsin, USA. All rights reserved. Scripture quotations marked NLT are taken from the Holy Bible, New Living Translation, copyright 1996, 2004, 2015. Used by permission of Tyndale House Publishers., Wheaton, Illinois 60189. All rights reserved. All emphasis within Scripture quotations is the author's own. Please note that Destiny Image's publishing style capitalizes certain pronouns in Scripture that refer to the Father, Son, and Holy Spirit, and may differ from some publishers' styles. Take note that the name satan and related names are not capitalized. We choose not to acknowledge him, even to the point of violating grammatical rules.

DESTINY IMAGE® PUBLISHERS, INC.
P.O. Box 310, Shippensburg, PA 17257-0310
"Promoting Inspired Lives."

This book and all other Destiny Image and Destiny Image Fiction books are available at Christian bookstores and distributors worldwide.

Cover design by Eileen Rockwell
Interior design by Terry Clifton

For more information on foreign distributors, call 717-532-3040.
Reach us on the Internet: www.destinyimage.com.

ISBN 13 TP: 978-0-7684-5142-9
ISBN 13 eBook: 978-0-7684-5143-6
ISBN 13 HC: 978-0-7684-5145-0
ISBN 13 LP: 978-0-7684-5144-3

For Worldwide Distribution, Printed in the U.S.A.
1 2 3 4 5 6 7 8 / 24 23 22 21 20

Contents

Foreword

By Patricia King

I love reading stories in the Bible about David—the great warrior king of Israel. David conquered many enemies as he constantly contended for victory on behalf of God's plans and desires for His people.

Obviously, he didn't simply wake up one morning, look in the mirror, and declare, "Wow, I'm a skilled warrior; I think I will go and slay a giant today." No, he was groomed by God Himself in the secret place. He knew the key to being a successful warrior.

It appears that David was somewhat rejected by his family in that they didn't give the impression that they esteemed, valued, or regarded him. When Samuel came to his family's house to anoint the next king from among Jesse's sons, David wasn't even considered to stand with his brothers. He was still out tending the sheep and wasn't invited to the lineup. As Samuel looked over each of David's brothers, he knew that the Lord's anointed was not before him. "Are there any more sons?" he asked.

I'm sure David's father had to ponder before responding with hesitation, "Hmmm, well, there's little David out in the field but…"

"Bring him in now," Samuel ordered.

So they called David in from the field and when he stood before Samuel, the prophet knew by the Spirit that God's warrior king was truly standing before him—this was the one he had come to anoint. That day, David was anointed as king but not yet appointed, so back to the fields with the sheep he went.

That isolated field was a holy place for him where he learned the "warrior's dance"—his rhythm with God. When the lions and the bears came to devour the sheep, the Lord empowered him to take them out with his bare hands. It was in that field where David learned to live before the audience of One. It was in that field where he learned the skill of the warrior. In that field, he learned the character of the warrior, and in that field of isolation he learned the dance of the warrior.

All the character attributes that were formed in David and all the seasoned skills he possessed as he later engaged in great battles were groomed in him while in the secret place, alone in the field with God. We see this amazing warrior slay a giant, conquer kingdoms, and overcome horrific obstacles and circumstances.

He was a "warrior man" fully yielded and submitted to his warrior God, but he was also very much a "dancing man." When David successfully brought the ark back to Jerusalem, he stripped off his kingly garments and external regalia and danced before the Lord with all his might in purity of spirit. This was the "warrior's dance"—birthed in the very presence and promises of God—oh, he truly knew the dance.

David's secret for becoming a great king was intimate acquaintance in God's presence, character, and nature—that is where he learned to dance and that is where he learned to war.

In *The Warrior's Dance*, Ana Werner will take you on a journey of discovering the attributes of who you are as God's warrior and the movements of the warrior's dance as you face challenges and obstacles in life. As David was groomed in the secret place, so also will you be as God forms you into a beautiful warrior whose very life becomes a delightful dance before the Lord.

Rise up warrior—and dance.

The Vision That Started It All

There are two scriptures that have always stuck out to me as I think about spiritual warfare:

> *Your hand-to-hand combat is not with human beings, but with the highest principalities and authorities operating in rebellion under the heavenly realms. For they are a powerful class of demon-gods and evil spirits that hold this dark world in bondage* (Ephesians 6:12 TPT).

> *In the world you have tribulation, but take courage; I have overcome the world* (John 16:33).

These verses point to the truth that we are in a battle, but through Christ we are not defeated. If you are a believer and are walking with the Lord, the darkness of this world does not like the light you carry.

Christians tend to have one of two beliefs when it comes to spiritual warfare. The first belief is that through the resurrection of Christ we have gained complete victory and access to Heaven. By His stripes we have been healed, and we can walk in freedom. That's truth!

Although I believe this is completely true, there is a danger in it. We can become lethargic, believing that because Christ was victorious against the enemy we do not need to do our part in combat. Time and time again, I see such people getting hit by the schemes of the enemy, and they are almost inept in the face of his attacks. Yes, we carry Jesus within us and so can claim victory as His sons and daughters. It's our inheritance to walk in His light and freedom! But while the enemy is still here on earth, his main purpose is to do everything he can to steal this freedom and snuff out the light of Christ. So if you are stepping out and bringing the light of Christ to a darkened world, you will experience resistance from the enemy. His main goal is to silence your voice and hold you in oppression. (More on this later.)

Then there is the other belief I have seen many camp out in. Everything seems to be warfare. Can you think of someone like this? The enemy is always out to get them, and they are constantly in battle mode. It's true that there is a battle, but the problem with this mindset is that it often wrongfully sees the enemy and his demons as so much larger than our God. Scripture says:

> *The God of peace will soon crush Satan under your feet. The grace of our Lord Jesus be with you* (Romans 16:20).

Although the enemy comes to steal, kill, and destroy our freedom, healing, and light, the *Lord reigns!* No demon is larger than God. Our focus should not be set on the enemy's attacks but on Christ Jesus who reigns over all. (More on this later, too.) But to pretend that there is no ongoing spiritual war is ignorant.

So then, what do we do as light-bearers in a darkened world to overcome the enemy through Christ Jesus? I had a recent vision about this:

The Warrior's Vision

I saw myself soaring over a landscape with Jesus. As I soared closer, He showed me a battlefield. I could see hundreds upon thousands of people fighting in a battle against demonic, oppressive spirits. They were all on the ground fighting from a position of defense. The oppressive spirits were bigger and stronger than the people, and the people were losing. Then I saw the King of Glory, Jesus Himself, dressed in His royal robes, ride up on a huge white horse. "Rise up!" He commanded the people. Suddenly, horses appeared for every person on the field, and I saw the people mount the horses, dressed in completely new armor. They were ready to win this battle.

"You are not under the curse, but above it. Find your weaponry, for you have lost it." Looking at the battlefield, I realized that I was marching. *Why am I marching?* I thought. Before me was a clash of power. I saw the enemy's workers sending out assaults against the King's soldiers. I saw the Lord's warrior angels fighting the demonic forces to protect the King's beloved ones there.

As the battle thickened, my spiritual ears opened and I could hear the sound of battle—the clash of swords upon swords, shields smashing against armor, shrieks of pain as people's bodies were wounded by the enemy's arrows and claws, and also shrieks as the demons were stabbed and overcome by the King's army. Back and forth, back and forth the battle continued.

Then, a loud alarm shrieked. The sound was disgusting! I felt instantly nauseated when I heard it. It was unlike any earthly sound I have ever heard. For a brief moment, I saw the enemy seated on a nasty-looking beast, and then his image shifted away. He could move and change form with ease. After that moment, I couldn't trace him with my eyes, but I could feel his presence still there leading his army. But he was hidden from my sight.

When that alarm sounded, I felt terror pulse through my body so much that I couldn't move. Fear paralyzed me. The King's army scattered in disarray. As soldiers were separated from the group, I saw how they became more vulnerable to the enemy's attacks. Smaller demons rose up and could pick them off one by one.

Then I heard the King's voice: "Time to release the drummers, Ana. Set the beat. Give the direction for My beloveds. We've gotten off course. Shift your focus. We are winning! Find the beat of My heart. Find the pulse of Holy Spirit and stay with it. Rise up. Grow louder in your declarations and prayers. Don't you know the power of prayer? As you step into the authority My Son has given to you, the sound of Heaven is released."

Then I was marching in the front line of battle, carrying a drum. In the natural, I have no idea how to play the drums. But I found myself in Heaven, setting a beat. I was hearing the sound from the Father and repeating it back on my little instrument. It was slow and steady at first, and then as the army of Christ joined with me it grew *loud* and faster. Our sound broke louder than the clash of the enemy's assaults. And we grew strong! I learned to tune my ears to listen more to the sound that the Father was making than the battle that was happening before me, and I could match His beat. We became victorious as we matched His sound. The enemy's army had to back off.

You and I are part of the end-time warrior Bride who is marching on the front lines of the battlefield. The enemy is scared of you! Do you know that? The Lord is raising us up to be a fearless Bride, recklessly abandoned to and in love with Jesus. Now it is time for us to rise up and pick up our weapons and march against the enemy as the warriors we were created to be.

Chapter 1

The Dance of a Pure Heart

Although purity is often discussed in terms of sexuality or freedom from sin, I wish to address a pure heart here in a different manner. The Lord showed me that He is raising up warriors who carry pure hearts before the Lord—unhindered by offense and unforgiveness.

The Offense-less Land of the Living

It was just an average day—nothing special about it, really. I asked the Lord to encounter me and interrupt my day. I was sitting outside on our back porch, journal ready for an encounter.

Suddenly, He broke in. Just like that, I was in a different location. In the vision, I could see a herd of wild horses galloping around joyfully. I watched them at first in wonderment at just how large and powerful they were. It was as I continued to watch them that I noticed another horse off in the distance, struggling alone. Curiosity impelled me to examine the struggle. Coming closer, I saw that this horse had a muzzle over its mouth. As I asked the Lord why the muzzle was on it, and the word *offense* appeared written across the muzzle.

Then I heard, "I have called the body of Christ to know freedom. To love and receive love freely, and to run with Me. You're in it for the ride with Me. You can't have anything restraining you. Offense is a restraint to receiving My glory. It will block the flow. Offense holds you back from all that I have for you." For me, that was the first time I had ever heard that offense blocks the flow of the Holy Spirit.

I've heard it said that offense reveals the heart. It's easy to get offended isn't it? Especially when we live in such a broken world. The enemy is constantly finding opportunities to test the offense level of our heart. And there are plenty just from other people who know and love Jesus! Then you turn on the news, hear or see something you should not, bump into someone abrasive in the grocery store—the list goes on and on of opportunities for offense to rise.

In this book on spiritual warfare, I want to address the subject of offense. It is an issue running rampant within the church yet is rarely spoken about. It is one of the enemy's strongest footholds in the present day.

Moral standards are leaving the church, and we lack the ability to draw a line in the sand over what we will and will not allow. At the same time, our offenses are also reaching a new high. Have we become too entitled? We are living in a generation that is now, more than ever, an "I *can* through Christ in me" generation! We are becoming an unstoppable force for God as we understand more and more who it is we carry inside of us. But every coin has a flip side. Are we also becoming a little too entitled, a little too easily offended, and a little less quick to forgive? Where is the balance of holding on to morals and yet extending grace in the church?

Offense in the Church

Our offenses quickly reveal the condition of our heart. I am convinced that the Lord looks at how we react to things. Perhaps the day's small chances for offense to arise are not something you find yourself struggling with. You are able to brush off the abrasive attempts of the enemy to cause offense. Perhaps you walk with some maturity under your belt.

But how about with leadership in the church? Do you possibly find yourself struggling with the thought that you could lead the ship better?

Offense within the ministry is one of the least spoken-about topics in modern Christianity. Every day, leaders, pastors, and prophets have church members ready to bury them with accusatory words. "That service Sunday, did you hear what he said?" "Why did she handle that situation like that? I would have handled it differently." The list goes on and on of accusations either said out loud or in our heart.

A Jezebel spirit is raging against church and ministry leaders (see 1 Kings 19). At her core, Jezebel believes she can direct the ship better. She questions why the Lord has placed that person over her in leadership. We've all been there.

You might also find yourself on the other side of this conversation as the pastor or ministry leader who has had offense thrown at you. I know I have. As someone who is a leader of a healing ministry, I am constantly asking the Lord for direction and wisdom to steer the ship, to encourage, to build up and train my team. But I make mistakes. I'll be first to admit that I'm not always right; I have a lot to learn.

One time I made the mistake of carelessly forgetting something that I was supposed to bring to a Tuesday night healing room. It was something small, but to one of our team members it was significant. After having a crazy day with my kids leading up to healing rooms that evening (as seems to always be the case), I had carelessly forgotten about the item. That team member instantly extended forgiveness, but I couldn't miss the disappointment on their face. I made a mistake. I was the first to admit it, but truth be told I felt like I had to re-prove myself as a leader who is worthy and dependable.

Extending grace to imperfect leadership shows maturity and also honor. If a Pastor or leader is sinfully doing something wrong, then obviously with wisdom there must be action taken to correct this. In our generation though, honor is not highly valued. We like correction, but do we like to honor? Have we lost a sense of God-given authority? God placed my pastor at the head of my church. He's not perfect, and yet I honor him and respect him and extend grace where grace is needed.

Prayer for Offense Toward Leadership

> *Lord right now, I ask you to show me if there was ever a time that I've been offended at a leader or person of authority in a church or ministry. God, if there is a place of hurt with this person, I ask you to come now and minster healing to my heart. I repent for ever cursing the leadership you placed before me, by: using my words to speak negatively of them, by thinking negative thoughts about them, or even believing that I could lead better. Father I repent and ask your forgiveness for not blessing my leaders more. Would you bless their lives God in this very moment. I pray you would rebuild communications and understanding between myself and them. They are not perfect, but Lord I choose to still bless them. Amen."*

As Jesus' final act before facing the brutality of the cross, He bowed low and washed His disciples' feet.

> *Jesus, knowing that the Father had given all things into His hands, and that He had come forth from God and was going back to God, got up from supper, and laid aside His garments; and taking a towel, He girded Himself. Then He poured water into the basin, and began to wash the disciples' feet and to wipe them with the towel with which He was girded* (John 13:3-5).

Servanthood is the upside-down kingdom. Submission is honored by God. It's not enough to submit in the act; the Lord values the submission of your heart's attitude.

My heart's attitude is an act of worship, an offering to the King. If I hold on to offense, whether with leadership or anyone else I might brush up against, I cannot offer up a pure offering to the King. It's tainted. It is like drinking sweet poison. Although staying offended may taste better and seem to satisfy the soul more at first, in the end it destroys the goodness and fullness of life He has for you.

Pure love always costs, but the King is so worth the cost. It's a sacrifice to extend undeserved forgiveness.

The Unoffended Heart

I'll never forget the morning we were robbed. It was just days before my husband and I were to leave for California to visit my family for the Thanksgiving holiday. We had planned and talked about this trip for so long, and anticipation was in the air. My husband Sam woke up early on a Saturday morning and thought to surprise me by going out and getting us coffee and pastries for breakfast. (My hunter and gatherer!) To his surprise, he looked out our living room window and discovered our car was missing. *Gone!*

"Hon, did you park the car somewhere else last night?" he called to me from the living room.

"No, what are you talking about?" was my sleepy response.

"It's gone. The car's not here!"

I bolted out of bed at light speed. (Well, it seemed like it for a non-morning person like myself.) "What do you mean it's gone?" I responded.

"It's gone, hon. It's *not here!*"

Our world suddenly blurred into a feeling of disbelief, then fear, then grief. When we had returned to the States from being missionaries in Nepal, we had been gifted this car as a huge answer to prayer. Now our gift, our beautiful blessing of a car was stolen!

There we were that morning with an empty driveway before us. As we dealt with the police report and phone call after phone call, I could feel the tears that I had been trying to choke back begin to leak their way out.

After everything with the police had finally quieted down, Sam and I stood in our living room hand in hand. I looked through tears into my husband's face and said, "Our response to all of this is being tested right now." Right then and there we vowed to not get offended despite the loss of our gift. We spent time praising and thanking God for who He was to us.

During the next few days that followed, it was extremely hard to hold our ground and remain true to that vow. It turned out that our car was stolen in the middle of the night from our driveway and used to haul a methamphetamine lab. Our car was found by the police in a neighboring state a few days after we left for our trip. It reeked of alcohol and cigarette smoke. The inside was full of stains from who knows what. In retrospect, it was only a silly car. We still had our lives and each other. But it wasn't the object that disturbed us; it was the helpless feeling of being robbed that was hard to swallow. Our safe neighborhood suddenly didn't feel so safe anymore. We had to pay hundreds of dollars to get our car back, which at the time was a stretch for our pocketbooks.

"I won't get offended," I kept telling myself through those days.

I was reminded of this incident again over one year later as red and blue lights flashed behind me and the police pulled me over to the side of the road.

"Ma'am, are you aware that this vehicle is reported as a stolen vehicle?" the police officer asked me as she approached my car.

"Mom, are you going to get ticket?" my four-year-old daughter piped up from the backseat.

Remain calm, I thought to myself. *What is happening?* The next statement really surprised me.

"Ma'am, are you aware that it is a federal offense to be driving a stolen vehicle and have children in the backseat? That's an amber alert," the officer quickly said. She then started to talk into her radio, "I'm going to need some backup."

An amber alert! I thought to myself. *They think I've stolen this vehicle and my children? What in the world is happening?* I quickly began to pray.

"Backup" turned out to be the chief of police, who showed up within one minute, gun drawn, approaching my car. With hands up in the air, I quickly started rattling off my husband's birthdate, social security number, and anything else I could remember. I explained what had happened with the vehicle the year before, and the mystery was solved. Our vehicle had been found in a different jurisdiction, and that jurisdiction had forgotten to file their paperwork. So our car was still showing up as a stolen vehicle.

Offense with God

At the end of the day, it wasn't my offense with the guys who had stolen our car that I had to deal with. My offense was with God. The question, "Why did we have to go through this?" kept rattling through my mind. *Did we do something to deserve this? Why didn't You prevent it, Lord?*

The days that followed our car being stolen felt like trying times. We were just waiting, hoping, and praying, but our questions weren't answered. What were we going to do? Buying a new car was simply just not an option for us. We came back to the States with very little. Trusting God to provide everything we needed was the only option.

Why do bad things happen to good people? The question will be there till the very end of the age. What I have come to realize is that this is not really the question to be asked. The real question is, what will be your character in that firing time? What will be your stance?

God is good, all the time, no matter what. It's irrevocable. In a time of real spiritual battle, in a time of waiting for the breakthrough, or even after a time of real loss, whether or not we will become offended with Him will be put to the test.

What will be your character in that firing time?

David's trust in the Lord was put to the test many times as King Saul chased after him and tried to kill him.

> *Heed the sound of my cry for help, my King and my God. ...In the morning, O Lord, You will hear my voice; in the morning I will order my prayer to You and eagerly watch* (Psalm 5:2-3).

No matter what, God is for you—not against you. It may not feel like it from what you can see with your natural eyes right now. But God is good, independent of our situations. He is Love manifested. He is our defender and upholder. Ultimately, our response has to be, "I will remain unoffended at Your timing and Your ways even though I might not understand them."

The unoffended heart is perhaps one of the hardest concepts to understand. It holds its ground by saying, "No matter what, God, I will love You. No matter the loss, no matter the pain." It is the walk to the cross. But we know the end of that story. We know that Jesus was victorious as He took back the keys of Hades from satan. We have the victory in Him.

Navigating Through Loss

However, having our car stolen wasn't the hardest test of my love and trust in God. I lost something much more. Sadly, I lost our son. Our world had been literally flipped upside down as we moved from the mission field of our rice paddy village in Nepal to the Midwest in the States. We had just come back, were in complete culture shock, and were living with my family at the time. And then we found out I was a few weeks pregnant with our first child. I was scared out of my mind with the thought of being a new parent.

Within days of discovering we were going to be parents, we shared our exciting news with our family. Then, three days later, I lost the baby. Miscarriage is a devastating thing many women go through. It's actually more common than people think. I'll never forget seeing that little fetus, praying, weeping over him, and burying my son. I never wish to revisit that day.

Grief

Where are You, God? Why? These questions continually passed through my mind in those days of grief. Everything slowed down. I remember thinking that it seemed like everyone around us was moving at a different pace, while my husband and I seemed to be trudging through our days as if we were underwater. Grief was swallowing us. This was a major disappointment with God that I had to take up with Him.

As grief kept pressing down on me like a thick x-ray blanket, I found all I could pray was, "God please help. I hurt." Have you been there? Maybe miscarriage isn't the road you have traveled down, but grief can be for anything. We all face loss at some point in life.

So, how do we navigate through loss? We need a compass that points us to the light during periods of the swallowing darkness of loss. I learned three things during my post-miscarriage time:

Number 1: It's okay to feel pain.

It is actually the healthiest thing you can do. There is much to be learned through the process of loss, but most of us would rather just move past it. Why go through pain when I can move right past it, right? My daughter is healing right now from contact with poison ivy we discovered in our backyard. Covering up the itchy rash with bandages to avoid the weird stares doesn't actually fix it. Letting it dry out is the best healing process.

That painful season of life, as I faced many tears, brought up some real raw moments between me and the Lord. I learned to cry out to Him—like *really* cry! Raw questions came to surface: "Where are You, God? What am I doing back here in the States? What's Your purpose for my life, God? I truly feel so lost right now! My husband and I are polar opposites…." You know, the questions that come up when all our crutches have been stripped away. Loss has a way of doing that.

As I leaned into God during that time of loss and really allowed myself to grieve, He came to me. Some days it would be in the sweet form of a surprise blessing. Other times, I would have a vision of just being held by the Father. He stroked my hair, washed my tears, and told me it would be okay and that He was here. He didn't necessarily answer my endless questions. Rather, He provided the strength I needed to face any loss or any battle. His strength was more than I bargained for, but was better than answers.

I learned to trust again, even through pain. I am convinced that if there are two things that the enemy is after more than anything else, they are our *trust* in God and our adoration of Him alone. That trust cannot be shaken. *No matter what!* That's where He is taking His seasoned Bride. She will be able to stand any shaking, any firing, and say, "No matter what, *I trust You* and love You. No matter what."

> That's where He is taking His seasoned Bride. She will be able to stand any shaking, any firing, and say, "No matter what, *I trust You* and love You. No matter what."

Number 2: I came face to face with my own entitlement.

What came to the surface in my grief was a very offended question: "How could You do this, God? How could You allow this to happen?"

Have you ever been there yourself? Can you relate? Something unexpected happens that seems to feel like the carpet was swept out from under your legs, and suddenly the question comes up: "How could You?" I call it the entitlement spirit, which says, "You can't do that to me!"

Our loving Father in Heaven does not want us to be in pain. There is no pain in Heaven. There is no loss in Heaven. Only joy. But we live in a painful, broken, fallen world.

Facing my own "how could You" forced me to correct my wrong belief that I was immune to bad experiences. Instead of remaining frustrated with God and blaming Him, I learned to blame the devil and the sin of this world and lean into God all the more. I found Him to be my fortress in those moments. There are not many things we can control, but our response to events in life is entirely our responsibility. That's the mark of a mature Bride. Truth be told, maturity doesn't come without testing.

Maturity doesn't come without testing.

I am reminded of this simple truth every time I lovingly correct my children. "When your brother pushes you for no reason, your response shouldn't be to push him back harder! What would be something better you could do?"

What will be your response to the setbacks? How will you navigate through the setbacks as they come? This question leads me to the third truth I learned through loss:

Number 3: Let go of disappointments.

This is perhaps one of the most important processes we can walk through for our healing. Disappointment and loss can hit us all at different levels and in different stages of life. The more I held on to my disappointment with God over the loss of our son, the more grief seemed to swallow me.

Letting go is a process! It's pretty rare to find someone who can let go of a major disappointment overnight. When our expectations aren't met, major disappointment can set in.

I eventually learned that the only way to deal with my disappointments was to just lay them down. "God, I thought this…but this happened. I lay it down at Your feet and ask You to take my disappointment. Will You come fill this hole I feel?" That simple prayer to God brought me perhaps the greatest breakthrough. Handing Him my disappointments brought the greatest peace. In my frailty, I found His strength. He became my rock when the ground felt shifty.

If you need to let go of a disappointment in your life, I invite you to pray this prayer:

> *God, I believe You are still good no matter what I am going through right now. I know that You love me. Help me find my way out of this valley. I choose to keep loving You and to rise above what I am going through right now. You are my strength. Renew my mind; renew my heart. Come love on me today, Lord. Help me to find You in the middle of all this. God, I don't have all the answers, but I know that You are leading me. I love You, Lord, no matter what. Amen.*

The Fragrance of Forgiveness and the Valley of Dry Bones

God is raising up a pure Bride who is unoffended and extends forgiveness easily.

Growing up, my mother and I didn't always have the most peaceful relationship. We had disagreements caused by natural life circumstances and personality differences. Later, we both went through inner healing to repair and restore our relationship. Now, we are both comfortable and can openly can talk about misunderstandings we had in the past. My mom is actually one of my closest friends now. Our story is a real testimony of how God can redeem a relationship and bring healing, so I hope it brings hope to someone reading this. I dare share something so personal here, because I believe someone reading this right now is walking through a tumultuous relationship that needs healing. Have hope! God has done a wonder in bringing restoration to my mother and my relationship, and He can in your's too! I pray that God begins the process of restoration in your relationships today.

When my husband and I were in Mozambique doing the Iris school of ministry with Heidi and Rolland Baker, one day I had a huge revelation downloaded to me about the fragrance that is released through forgiveness.

I became really sick. All my life, I had been prone to infections in my throat, and I got another one. The infection had spread quite quickly, and my right tonsil was swollen like a golf ball. Praying, I asked the Lord, "God, why do I always get infections in my throat? I'm getting sick of this battle. Would You show me what's going on?"

Then wow! Did He do an unexpected thing! I was instantly taken up into a very powerful vision. I found myself walking through a valley of bones. Everywhere I looked, I could see bones that looked dried and cracked. "Where have You taken me, Lord?" I asked as I looked around.

Then He spoke loudly. "I am showing you a place where you are still holding on to pain. We have to go here Ana. It's time to wash this valley clean." The Lord then showed me that although I had gone through healing from past pain, there were still places in my heart holding the pain.

"You are right, Lord. I've forgiven my mother, but there is a little bit of me that is still holding on to the pain. God, I choose to let go of the pain now and let go of any lingering bitterness and unforgiveness. I choose to walk the path of forgiveness and freedom," I prayed.

Then, with Holy Spirit's nudge, I found myself saying out loud,"Right now, I break any agreement that I had made with a victim spirit way back when I was a little girl." (More on breaking agreements later.)

Just then, I was taken in the vision and saw a dam above the valley burst open and flooding waters pour through the valley. It was the most beautiful and freeing vision! The waters, which represented the Father's love, gushed through that valley and washed away all of the bones. Then I came out of the vision and discovered that my throat was completely healed.

As I reached for my neck in shock and felt that the golf-ball-sized tonsil was no longer swollen, I heard the voice of the Lord in that moment say, "It's done." Flipping open my Bible, my eyes fell on Ezekiel 37.

> *"Our bones are dried up and our hope has perished. We are completely cut off." Therefore prophesy and say to them, "Thus says the Lord God, 'Behold, I will open your graves and cause you to come up out of your graves, My people; and I will bring you into the land of Israel.*

Then you will know that I am the Lord, when I have opened your graves and caused you to come up out of your graves, My people. I will put My Spirit within you and you will come to life, and I will place you on your own land. Then you will know that I, the Lord, have spoken and done it,' declares the Lord" (Ezekiel 37:11-14).

I believe the Lord was showing me how unforgiveness and holding on to pain is truly a grave to our souls. It ultimately robs us of living with fullness of life in our promises from the Father. Unforgiveness and holding on to bitterness opens a door of access for the enemy and gives him permission to come and attack us with sickness.

Let us warriors not forget the ultimate forgiveness that we are all so underserving of but have freely received from the Father. No sin is so large that He won't forgive. We are created in the image of Christ, and that means we must fight our flesh and extend forgiveness. Holding on to unforgiveness and pain will only hurt us in the end.

God spoke to me recently in a vision. He said, "I am removing the badges of survival from My beloved, which so many are wearing, and I am replacing them instead with the fragrance of forgiveness."

Let us all, then, release this fragrance of forgiveness freely as a true testimony of the love of Christ. May all us warriors learn the dance of purity—living with love clothed and wrapped around our necks; untainted by sin, offense, unforgiveness, or bitterness. Let us learn to dance freely with pure love as our shield.

Chapter 2

The Dance of Contending

The Great Crossing Over

You're on the brink of crossing over into the promised land. Can you feel it? Do you feel that urgency in your spirit right now? Your promise from God for which you have been contending for so long is that close. Maybe today you feel as most mothers in labor feel during those final pushes before their beautiful baby makes its entrance into this world. I remember at 22 hours of labor I thought, "God, I may die today. I'm ready for Heaven. Just take me!" And then that beautiful, small cry pierced the sounds and exhaustion of the room—my daughter's first expression of her voice.

You're that close.

Do you think the Israelites felt this urgency at each setback they experienced? From slavery to each horrific plague that hit Egypt to the Passover. Then came the crossing of the Red Sea, and then they spent 40 years in the desert. *When are You coming, Lord? When will we fully gain our freedom and enter the promised land?* may have been their cry!

Maybe you find yourself in this very place today. You have been waiting and standing on a promise of God for a long time now. Your cry might be, *Where are You, God, and when are You going to move?*

Time to Push

There is a time and season to rest, and there is a season to push and contend. It's important to hear from the Lord to know what season you're in. If you feel like you are up against setback after setback, perhaps it is because your breakthrough is right around the corner. I prophecy to you right now, friend—*don't quit!*

I can't tell you how many times my husband and I have walked through what felt like mountains of shut doors, disappointments, confusion, restlessness, direct attacks of the enemy, and hopelessness to finally get to our breakthrough moment and look back and say, "Ahhh, it all makes sense now."

The Lord has shown me that part of a warrior's dance is in this place of contending.

Our Testimony of Contending *Until*

Recently, the Lord showed us that it was time for our family of four to move out of our rental home and purchase our own home. We marveled at the idea at first, but we quickly became discouraged by how unrealistic it seemed.

One day, I heard Him ask me to pray specifically for what I wanted, which is a key the Lord has shown me that often helps me get my breakthrough. So I waited on Holy Spirit, and then I prayed, "God, I pray that You would give us an inherited estate that a family member does not want and so is willing to sell at a great price. I would like it to have lots of light, because I love light, and also have an office already established for me upstairs with plenty of light."

After I released that prayer request, God sent some confirmation to encourage me that He had heard my prayers. The Lord continued to send me prophetic words about this house.

The Mailer Room

Do you know that there is a mail room in Heaven? I wrote about it in my first book, *The Seer's Path*, but often the Lord brings me back to it to remind me of the importance of petitioning Heaven.

One day the Lord brought me into a room of Heaven. In it I saw rows and rows of parcels lining the walls. As far as my eyes could see, down and up, those parcels waited. The room was busy with angels bustling back and forth, grabbing these parcels and carrying them down to earth at the direction of Jesus.

What caught my attention in that room the most was that some of the angels were just standing and waiting along the sides of the room. Disturbed, I asked Jesus, "What are they doing?"

He responded to me, "They are taking answers to the prayers of saints down below. Each one is specifically assigned for the delivery of these special packages." Those who were not busy were waiting for a believer to pray and ask! It took my prayer language up an entire notch from that day forward as I realized the power of my prayers.

Matthew 7:7-8 says:

> *Ask, and the gift is yours. Seek, and you'll discover. Knock, and the door will be opened for you. For every persistent one will get what he asks for. Every **persistent seeker** will discover what he longs for. And everyone who knocks persistently will one day find an open door* (TPT).

Can you imagine? What if your breakthrough hasn't come yet because you didn't ask or because you stopped petitioning Heaven?

So back to my story of how contending brought breakthrough. After I had prayed that specific prayer for our house, three different prophets came through our area and all prophesied to me the exact thing I had asked God for!

"I believe there is an inherited estate the Lord has for you that will be your place to move to," was the word spoken over and over. *Wow God!*

So we began looking for a house, and then we found it. The exact place I had prayed into existence—an inherited estate that a family member was willing to sell at a low price to get off their hands, with lots of light and an already established office.

But no bank would give us a loan. The house was an old home and a total rehab. No bank wanted to take the risk with it. We tried literally every bank. As I left to go pick my daughter up for school one day, our last option called my husband and said no.

But I just couldn't shake the promise of this house off me. "God, I just don't feel like this is a closed door from You. In the natural it looks that way, but, God, you told us that this was our house. You are going to do a miracle that is beyond what I can see. God, would You move this mountain for us? We have done everything we know to do."

At that exact moment of discouragement, my husband was in his office at our home. A card fell onto his keyboard out of a stack of business cards he had received. "You didn't come this far to only come this far," it read.

"God's going to do something. Somehow, we are going to get this house," we both kept saying to each other. The next day was the last day for us to make a counteroffer on the house. So time was of the essence. We left that night to go direct our healing rooms, still with no loan approval.

As we drove to the healing rooms, I heard the voice of the Father: "I am a God of the impossible. You've done your part; now watch what I am about to do. I am a God of the last-minute miracles!"

I excitedly shared with my husband what God had just shared with me, and we chose to grab hands and pray it in. "Let's pray in that last-minute breakthrough," I said to my husband. And, boy, did we pray!

Ten minutes later, a prophetic friend of mine sent me a text: "God is a God of the last-minute breakthroughs!" Wow, what a confirmation!

And guess what? *He did it!* At the very last minute, a bank reexamined our finances and decided to take a risk and grant us the loan we needed. It was literally down to the last minute! Not only did we face discouragement from the banks, but even as we were trying to process all the paperwork, the power company showed up and had to evacuate our family. A recent ice storm had ripped the electric box off our wall, so it was a fire hazard! Talk about contending *until* we saw the promise come through—to the very last minute!

But the promise came.

Use That Sword

Let's take a look at what Jesus did when He was under real spiritual warfare.

> *Then Jesus was led up by the Spirit into the wilderness to be tempted by the devil. And after He had fasted forty days and forty nights, He then became hungry. And the tempter came and said to Him...* (Matthew 4:1-3).

Before we read any further, let's stop and take note that the enemy came and tried to combat Jesus when Jesus had been weakened from fasting. Have you ever noticed that the enemy tries to come combat you when you are at a low or when you may have let your guard down? That's because he knows you are powerful, so he will try to come and hit you when you are down and at your weakest.

Back to Scripture:

> *Again, the devil took Him to a very high mountain and showed Him all the kingdoms of the world and their glory; and he said to Him, "All these things I will give You, if You fall down and worship me." Then Jesus said to him, "Go, Satan! For it is written, 'You shall worship the Lord your God, and serve Him only.'" Then the devil left Him; and behold, angels came and began to minister to Him* (Matthew 4:8-11).

I have been through battles and spiritual attacks, and it amazes me how slow I used to be at getting out my sword—the Word of God—and fight the enemy with it.

> *For the word of God is living and active and sharper than any two-edged sword* (Hebrews 4:12).

When this finally sank in, I came up with my battle-plan book. It's a book of scriptures I've written out that I can draw out when I feel like there is a real spiritual battle on. These scriptures have become dear to me. I stand on them, I meditate on them, and I try to memorize them. The point is, I am prepared to use my sword. The Word of God is active, alive, and the enemy will flee from it! Using Scripture is such a key in contending against the schemes of the enemy.

Here are just a few scriptures I have used before when I felt like I was in a real battle. I encourage you to build on them and add many more.

> *By His scourging we are healed* (Isaiah 53:5).
>
> *Moses built an altar and named it The Lord is My Banner* (Exodus 17:15).
>
> *So we are convinced that every detail of our lives is continually woven together to fit into God's perfect plan of bringing good into our lives, for we are his lovers who have been called to fulfill his designed purpose* (Romans 8:28 TPT).
>
> *For the Lord your God is the one who goes with you, to fight for you against your enemies, to save you* (Deuteronomy 20:4).
>
> *For the land, into which you are entering to possess it, is not like the land of Egypt from which you came, where you used to sow your seed and water it with your foot like a vegetable garden. But the land into which you are about to cross to possess it, a land of hills and valleys, drinks water from the rain of heaven, a land for which the Lord your God cares; the eyes of the Lord your God are always on it, from the beginning even to the end of the year* (Deuteronomy 11:10-12).
>
> *There is a river whose streams make glad the city of God, the holy dwelling places of the Most High. God is in the midst of her, she will not be moved* (Psalm 46:4-5).

But they shook off the dust of their feet in protest against them and went to Iconium. And the disciples were continually filled with joy and with the Holy Spirit (Acts 13:51-52).

He who believes in Me, the works that I do, he will do also: and greater works than these he will do; because I go to the Father. Whatever you ask in My name, that will I do, so that the Father may be glorified in the Son. If you ask Me anything in My name, I will do it (John 14:12-14).

And He got up and rebuked the wind and said to the sea, "Hush, be still." And the wind died down and it became perfectly calm (Mark 4:39).

Decree and Declare Again and Again!

Our decrees are like a partnership with Heaven. When God gives you a promise and you're up against a war, use the power of those promises to annihilate the enemy's attempts to take you out.

Once, I found myself face to face with the spirit of death. While I was on a ministry trip to New Orleans, my body started to go into all the symptoms of beginning to miscarry our baby girl. As I sat there and began to hemorrhage, and my body was having forced contractions, I could see the literal spirit of death in my room. Each time it approached me, the pain would only increase.

Mustering up the little strength I could, I began to worship and just call on the name of Jesus. As I did that, the demon inched back. The battle went on and on. I would gain a little ground and the pain would lessen; but then the spirit of death would lunge at me with another attack. I would worship and recite the Word of God to battle against that spirit of death. Finally, righteous anger came over me and I looked that ugly beast in the eyes and began to decree and declare the promises of God that the Lord had shown us about our daughter.

I declared and decreed to the enemy, "This baby will live a life where it walks in tremendous faith. This baby is mighty and carries an anointing of joy! It shall live in the name of the Lord. I will teach this baby to see in the spirit, and it will wreak havoc on you and all your friends!"

At that, the spirit of death completely vanished. The war over my baby's life was over, and to this day she is a beautiful, healthy, joyful six-year-old.

This wasn't my first time having to really use the weaponry of decreeing and declaring over a bleak situation, but I will admit that this encounter has most marked me.

Job 22:27-28 says, *"You will pray to Him, and He will hear you; and you will pay your vows. You will also decree a thing, and it will be established for you; and light will shine on your ways."*

As we decree and declare what God has promised to us, we are unleashing promises from Heaven. It activates our faith, and discouragement must flee. If a promise of God is written over your life in Heaven, then know it must come to be.

Scrolls of Heaven

*Then those who feared the Lord talked with each other,
and the Lord listened and heard. A scroll of remembrance was written in his presence concerning those
who feared the Lord and honored his name* (Malachi
3:16 NIV).

*"Look, I am coming soon! Blessed is the one who keeps
the words of the prophecy written in this scroll." I, John,
am the one who heard and saw these things. And when
I had heard and seen them, I fell down to worship at
the feet of the angel who had been showing them to me.
But he said to me, "Don't do that! I am a fellow servant
with you and with your fellow prophets and with
all who keep the words of this scroll. Worship God!"*
(Revelation 22:7-9 NIV)

Did you know there are scrolls of Heaven with your destiny
written on them? The Bible speaks of scrolls in Heaven, and
one day the Lord brought me into a vision. He led me into a
room where there were large drawing tables. Along the walls
were scrolls upon scrolls. I could see angels throughout the
room. Jesus nodded at an angel, and the angel went and got
one of my scrolls.

"Do you want to see yours?" Jesus smiled in excitement and
asked me.

"Yes! Please!" I responded.

I watched as the Lord then rolled out this huge scroll on the
long table. The page had gold edging. As I looked with Him
excitedly to see what was written, I watched in bewilderment as

pictures started showing up in gold on the page. I saw things that had already happened in my life, then a few things that were to come. As I tried to stare intently and make out the pictures of things in the future, which were blurry, Jesus blew on the scroll, and the gold dust fell on my chest.

"The destiny is written on your heart, beloved. Don't worry about knowing everything now," He said.

I felt the warm, tangible Presence of God rest over my heart on my chest, and it stayed with me all day even after the vision.

The destiny is written on your heart.

Biblical Decrees and Petitions that Changed History

Let's take a look at a few people from the Bible who changed the destiny of a people group by their petitions, decrees, and declarations.

David against Goliath:

> This day the Lord will deliver you into my hands, and I will strike you down...for the battle is the Lord's and He will give you into our hands (1 Samuel 17:46-47).

Queen Esther stands up for the Jewish people:

> *If it pleases the king and if I have found favor before him and the matter seems proper to the king and I am pleasing in his sight, let it be written to revoke the letters devised by Haman, the son of Hammedatha the Agagite, which he wrote to destroy the Jews who are in all the king's providences* (Esther 8:5).

These are just two biblical examples, and there are many more you can find as you dig into the scriptures.

So, how do we access these scrolls of Heaven? It is my belief that as we decree and declare the promises God has spoken over us, these scrolls are unrolled from the shelves.

Everything is in the timing of the Lord, obviously, but we can petition through our declarations, decrees, and partnership with the Presence of God to open those scrolls. Receiving prophetic words is amazing and so edifying. Let's move our position from just soaking them in to putting them to action. Put those prophecies into action. Target your prayers to bring in the prophecies!

Put those prophecies into action. Target your prayers to bring in the prophecies!

You have a promise over your life! If you have yet to know the purpose of God or the plans He has for you, you can at least claim this:

> *But I have come to give you everything in abundance, more than you expect—life in its fullness until you overflow!* (John 10:10 TPT)

Reminding God of His Promises

So let's go back to that story about our house. There I found myself with a decision to make. As I was driving to go pick up my daughter from school and that last bank option had just denied us the loan we needed for that house, what would be my stance or position? Trust me, defeat would have been the easy option.

But I decided to contend instead.

I remembered when God was so frustrated that He wanted to wipe the Israelites out. Moses reminded God of His promise to bless His people, and he changed God's mind (see Exod. 32:9-14).

I remembered when Jesus shared with His disciples about a widow who kept persistently asking a judge for his help and protection, and because of her persistence her petition was granted to her (see Luke 18:1-8).

"No," I heard myself praying out loud, "this is not a shut door. God, You said that this was to be our house. You showed me in dreams and prophecies. You even gave my husband a vision of us in the house. Even the exact street name has prophetic meaning for us. You told me that this would be my house of light, but that I would have to fight for it. God, would You move this mountain for us? You are a God of the last-minute miracle. Would You do a miracle now for our family, God?" Then I began praying in tongues. Praying in tongues is always a wonderful thing to do when you are facing any form of warfare or discouragement. Then I began to sing: "I believe in You, God, I believe in You. You're the God of miracles," I sang over and over.

The atmosphere in that car shifted from absolute discouragement to one saturated with faith. And *then* He broke through.

Perhaps you have been contending for so long that the idea of contending any longer almost seems to be the last thing you want. I implore you, *don't quit!* Breakthrough is right around the corner, knocking at the door. Can you hear it? I repeat, *can you hear it?* I pray for you, right now, for an increased measure of resistance toward discouragement and the ability to stand against the warfare and contend *until* for those promises of God over your life. Let our beat match the Father's beat. Let us match what the Father is saying and drown out the voice of the enemy on the battlefield.

No weapon that is formed against you will succeed; And every tongue that rises against you in judgement you will condemn. This [peace, righteousness, security + triumph over opposition] is the heritage of the servants of the LORD, And this is their vindication from Me. Says the LORD

Isaiah 54:17 AMP

Chapter 3

The Dance of Praise

I'm going to share with you an encounter in the throne room of Heaven that gave me the title for this book. My hope is that as you read this you will be taken right up into your own throne room encounter with Jesus.

The Throne Room Dance

One day, I saw myself in a vision right up in the throne room of Heaven. I was wearing a beautiful, spotless white wedding dress. I could see Jesus in the center of the room, but from afar. I began running toward Him, but the weird thing was that I kept looking back. That's when I noticed that instead of wearing gorgeous shoes to match the beauty of my wedding dress, I was actually wearing some old running shoes.

As I kept looking back, the feeling I had was that I just couldn't catch Jesus in this season and that I had to just catch my breath as I ran.

Next, I saw Jesus walk toward me. He extended His hands to me, and in them I saw a beautiful pair of ballet slippers.

"Dance through it. Worship and dance freely in the throne room," I heard Him say to me. So I took off my running shoes and replaced them with the slippers for dancing.

As I began to dance in the throne room, I saw and also felt the most bizarre thing. As I danced, bright and vibrant colors danced around me. I was moving with the wind of Holy Spirit's Presence, and it felt amazing. All sorts of different hues of colors were being released, and I was captivated by them as I danced.

The second thing was that I felt a bizarre change. There's that phrase *light as a feather*—well, that's how I felt. I felt light, just full of joy. Time seemed to stop as I danced and danced. Forgetting all the heaviness I was carrying previously from stresses of the day, I just danced, watching the colors and watching Jesus smiling at me.

"Oh, my King," I looked at Jesus, smiling. "I just love You."

I suddenly found myself face to face with Jesus. He was right there. Jesus then looked through me. He looked right into my eyes. Those eyes will just stop you in your tracks! His eyes were a beautiful sapphire blue color, but as I looked at them deeply I saw they were full of fire. Light seemed to glimmer and gleam right out of them. I have never seen eyes like this before in all my life. His eyes were alive and full of love.

Then He tenderly spoke to me.

"I see you. I see you," was all He said, but at that I was undone.

There is a scripture I love to meditate and chew on.

> *Enter his gates with thanksgiving and his courts with praise; give thanks to him and praise his name* (Psalm 100:4 NIV).

For so long, I have known this scripture in the New International Version. But look at it in *The Passion Translation*:

> *You can pass through his open gates with the password of praise. Come right into his presence with thanksgiving. Come bring your thank offering to him and affectionately bless his beautiful name!*

The *password* of *praise!* Wow! That does put things into perspective, doesn't it? Gates are the barriers that allow (or block) the passage or entrance of outsiders. But if you have a *key* to that gate, you can break through that barrier.

Our praise, worship, adoration, and thankfulness unlock our ability to step into a deeper measure of His Presence.

Taking Our Running Shoes Off

Another encounter I had with the Lord really encouraged me. One time, as I entered the throne room, I heard the Lord say, "Don't prove your value. Know it."

Now, don't read this wrong. I am not in any way prideful when I walk into the throne room. I know my place, which is always on my face in worship. I walk in as a humble child every time, no matter how much He teaches me before I enter. I know the authority I walk in, but my posture is always that of a learner.

I know the authority I walk in, but my posture is always that of a learner.

However, there is a place where understanding our true value to Jesus breaks all cords of fear off of us. You and I are so valuable to Jesus that He would face the cross and the horrific pain and anguish He went through just to bridge the gap between us and Heaven. He stepped off His throne in Heaven temporarily just to have relationship with you. You are that valuable.

That's the beauty of grace. Nothing I do or say could be enough to give me access to Heaven. The Bible says, "*For the wages of sin is death*" (Rom. 6:23). Yet He still looks at you with all your sinful ways, all your mistakes, and sees you are valuable and worth it.

There is no point in performing for Him because we don't have to. The keys of access have already been given to us through Jesus.

When I took off my running shoes in that vision, I realized that I had been trying to "run"—work myself up to His

Presence. Obviously, there are things that help us get into His Presence, such as reading His Word, fasting, praying in tongues, etc. But as I read back through my journal describing that encounter, I came across what He told me while I was taking off my running shoes. He said, "You're already in. You have access here."

See, I needed to stop running or performing *for* His Presence. I needed to just dance and worship *in* His Presence. There was a transformational shift there. Did you catch it? From *for* to *in*.

Abide in Me, and I in you (John 15:4).

So, warrior, worship out of a place of being with Him and loving Him. Move away from worshiping out of performance. The most anointed worship sets I have ever been a part of are those moments when the worship leaders forget the audience before them and just lets go and freely worship to the audience of one—Jesus. Like David *"leaping and dancing before the Lord"* (2 Sam. 6:16), let's praise and worship God freely. *The most dangerous warriors are those who are free and in love with the King!* To be fully free means to understand real love. God really loves you just as you are and doesn't demand performance from you.

Worship as Weaponry

Once the Lord took me into an encounter where I found myself in a room of Heaven where weapons lined the walls. Jesus motioned for me to pick one. As I looked at some awesome, heavy weaponry that looked like it could really do some damage (shields, swords with extra sharp ridges on the edges, metal helmets, etc.), none of them seemed right. Although these all looked amazing, none of them truly appealed to me. Then I saw it. I saw my weapon of choice. Hanging up amongst coats, I saw a shiny-looking dress similar to a knight's chain mail. As I looked closer at it, I saw there were pearls sewn all throughout it.

"You have chosen well, Ana," Jesus smiled at me. I looked at the pearls, wondering what their significance was. "Pearls are created out of friction. These are your times of sacrificial praise, when you worship and praise out of great conflict. Praise will be your weapon."

Now, I know many of us would rather have the huge sharp spear or axe to crush our enemies, but praise is one of the most powerful weapons. I have seen it put into use, and it really causes the enemy to shrink back.

In Second Chronicles 20 Jehoshaphat and the Israelites were going into battle against the sons of Ammon, Moab, and also some Meunites. The prophet Jahaziel gave Jehoshaphat a word: "*You need not fight in this battle; station yourselves*" (2 Chron 20:17). Look at their response!

> *Jehoshaphat bowed his head with his face to the ground, and all Judah and the inhabitants of Jerusalem fell down before the Lord, worshiping the Lord. The Levites, from the sons of the Kohathites and of the sons of the Korahites, stood up to praise the Lord God of Israel, with a very loud voice* (2 Chronicles 20:18-19).

Jehoshaphat then stationed the psalmists and worship leaders to go out before the army and lead with singing and praise. *"When they began singing and praising, the Lord set ambushes against the sons of Ammon, Moab and Mount Seir, who had come against Judah; so they were routed"* (2 Chron. 20:22). We can see here that the enemy was defeated through praise and worship! Did you hear that? The enemy was defeated through praise and worship!

Praise Shifts Everything

In the throne room of God, there is a constant state of worship. Revelation 4:8 says:

> *Each of the four living creatures had six wings, full of eyes all around and under their wings. They worshiped without ceasing, day and night, singing, "Holy, holy, holy is the Lord God, the Almighty! The Was, the Is, and the Coming!"* (TPT)

Every time I am granted access into the throne room, I immediately fall on my face and lay down and worship. The Presence coming from the throne of God is so thick, so weighty that it demands my lying-down posture. There is nothing like it. There is a righteous fear of the Lord that always comes over me when I am there. Jesus is our friend, and Holy Spirit is our counselor. But there is a righteous fear of God that needs to come back to the church. Righteous fear causes repentance. Its immediate response is to become purer before the Lord. The fear of the Lord creates in us the desire to become more like Him and reveals our own weakness. Every time I am in the Presence of God, I realize just how weak I am without Him, how much I need Him, and how much I want to look more like Him. You can't enter the throne room of God and leave unchanged. It's a righteous dipping.

> ## You can't enter the throne room of God and leave unchanged. It's a righteous dipping.

So in the throne room, where the Presence of God is the thickest, there is a constant state of worship and praise! Why? Praise and worship is an appropriate response to the Presence, and the Presence of God always comes when praise and worship is thick. I believe there is a distinct connection between the two.

Your worship shifts the atmosphere and brings the power of God to refresh, renew, and restore you! Do you know there is a spiritual atmosphere? As we worship, the fragrance of our worship is like a sweet perfume or offering to the Father that is lifted up straight to the throne room.

> *Are there any believers in your fellowship suffering great hardship and distress? Encourage them to pray! Are there happy, cheerful ones among you? Encourage them to sing out their praises!* (James 5:13 TPT)

In the footnotes of this scripture in *The Passion Translation* it says, "Or 'pluck the strings of a harp' or 'sing a psalm.'" I can't tell you the number of times I have been in a battle spiritually where I know the enemy is so strongly rising up against me, and yet my praise and worship breaks through the oppression.

Three Times the Atmosphere Was Shifted by *Praise*

While I can share many examples of times when I have used praise as my weaponry, I choose these three to share with you now because I believe these specifically will encourage someone reading this.

As a prophet, often the strongest warfare I actually have experienced (which might sound surprising,) has come from within the church—a religious spirit. A religious spirit comes to try and shut down a move of God or the prophetic voice. We can see that all the way back to when Jesus walked the earth, as the Pharisees continually questioned His ministry and tried to bring doubt and confusion to the people.

I dare share this story because I know that someone reading has recently felt like quitting the ministry and feels extremely discouraged as a religious spirit has come to try and take them out. Have hope! Worship will break the warfare!

My assistant and I were ministering at church one time, and the leader of the ministry asked to meet with me in private. I'll never forget the look on my assistant's face as the leader looked me straight in the eyes and told me, "I want you to pray this specific way only…." I politely excused myself, as I knew that although I disagreed with their actions, I still needed to respect and honor them as the leader of the church. My assistant and I went into the back office.

"We need to worship," I said. "Worship will break the power of the religious spirit that is here. It's time to praise."

After we worshiped for a good amount of time, we walked into that church to minister and the atmosphere had completely shifted. We were able to minister there with Holy Spirit freely without human control that evening, and many deliverances and healings occurred.

The second experience that I want to share with you happened to my husband and I in Africa. When we were in Mozambique as missionaries, my husband became sick with a staph infection in his blood that caused his stomach to bleed. Doctors told us that we might have to return home if they couldn't get the infection to stop and if Sam couldn't hold the medicine down. As he lay there moaning in our little hut and running an incredibly high fever, I went into the little communal kitchen next door to pray. I use the word *pray* loosely—really, I was crying out to God. "God what are You doing? What am I supposed to do? Please don't let him die! We don't want to have to go back to the States already; it's just not our time." I was there praying for a miracle in that little kitchen when I heard the voice of God audibly: "Go lay hands on him and sing the name of Jesus."

So I did. I tore into our little hut and told Sam what I was going to do. He moaned in agreement, unable to resist anything God told me to do at that point!

The strangest thing happened. All I sang was literally, "Jesus, Jesus, Jesus," as I placed my hands on his head. I continued, over and over, and realized suddenly that his forehead had become cool. *Wow!* I thought, *It's working!* I placed my hands then on his chest, which was still boiling hot with fever. Again I sang the name, "Jesus, Jesus, Jesus," and his temperature dropped. I continued all the way down to his feet, and the fever completely broke! Sam sat up, looking like he had been raised from the dead.

My last example of the power of using worship as a weapon is not about a physical attack from the enemy, but what I believe the enemy so often aims at first—our mind.

This attack came directly after a huge breakthrough. (On a side note, I've seen this time and time again. Often spiritual warfare thickens directly on the heels of promotion. It's the enemy's tactic to try and distract you.) I had just gone on Sid Roth's *It's Supernatural!* show for the second time, speaking on my second book and also ministering to the live audience there. As a bit of backstory, the first time I had been on the show, the day the show aired internationally, my husband woke up with half of his face paralyzed. Doctors called it Bell's palsy, but I just called it demonic. He fought that for six months and is almost completely healed now. So when invited onto the show for a second time, in the background of my head I thought, *Okay. I am not giving in to fear when this second show airs! My family is not going to be physically attacked again by the enemy. But I better get my intercessors geared up and really covering us as a family against any physical attacks.*

> **Often spiritual warfare thickens directly on the heels of promotion.**

Despite this, I was unprepared for the attack I experienced the day that second show aired. The battlefield was different this time. Rather than a physical attack on my health, the attack was more in my mind. Suddenly, I woke up that morning feeling complete discouragement. The discouragement I felt that week was unlike any discouragement I have ever felt. I suddenly went from feeling like, "Yes, God, I'll keep doing anything for You and I can change the world with Jesus," to, "Why am I even in ministry? Am I even making a difference? The ministry isn't really going that well. Am I even impacting lives? Maybe I should just stop prophesying and quit." Like a dark cloud following me around, suddenly I felt purposeless and very confused. Little did I know, many prophetic friends I had were going through the exact same thing in this season. A real assault of the enemy had been released on the prophets and pastors across this earth to try and discourage us and pull us off our destinies!

Maybe you are reading this right now and can relate to that. Someone reading this is experiencing this currently. Well, I want to encourage you—you can get free from this attack on your mind and ministry. Read on for what happened in my battle.

At 2 a.m. one night, I woke up in an ugly place. I could feel the spiritual oppression all around me, and yet I couldn't war it off. "God, in everything you've taught me, why can't I war this assault off? Help me, God!"

"Go worship," was all I heard back in response.

So I quietly slipped downstairs to my office where no one else could hear me while the house was sleeping. I put on my headphones and put on some worship music. There on the carpet I lay with my face between my folded hands, crying out to God. In that place of what felt like mental agony, I just began to worship. I sang and sang and sang. As I sang, suddenly it felt like the atmosphere changed in that little office. I could literally feel that oppressive spirit being tangibly pulled off of me, and I felt like I could breathe again. It was like the dark cloud that had been over my mind was lifting off and I could see light and truth again. I found myself being able to pull myself off the ground and dance again. My spirit was lifted up from a completely wrecked, discouraged place, to being able to focus my eyes on Jesus. As I just focused on Jesus, He came. In that moment, He spoke love over me, reaffirmed me in how He sees me, and reiterated direction, purpose, and destiny over me. Worship broke it. Worship cast that oppressive spirit off.

Worshiping through our situations, no matter how bleak they might look in the natural, causes us to lift our heads and shift our focus away from our problems and place it on Jesus. Shifting our focus away from the power of the enemy and turning it on to *how great* our God is, I believe, steals power from the enemy himself.

Focus Returned

We are not just physical beings; we are spiritual beings as well. Ephesians 6:12 says, *"For our struggle is not against flesh and blood, but against the rulers, against the powers, against the world forces of this darkness, against the spiritual forces of wickedness in the heavenly places."*

If you are not convinced that there is a spiritual realm, that should be a wake-up call. We are in a spiritual battle. I am convinced that the enemy's ultimate goal is to pull people away from intimacy with the King in whatever way he can. Distractions, oppression, sickness, offense, bitterness, sin, busyness, hurt, pain, wounding, unforgiveness, pride—the list goes on and on. All of these things can pull us away from remaining close to the Father. If the enemy can step in and create separation in our relationship with the King, between our trust and love for Him, he will try. Even our own lack of ability to receive love from Jesus can be a way the enemy tries to push us further away.

Not everything is a battle, though. We have to be careful that we don't focus our attention on all the works of the enemy. That's exactly what he wants! The enemy is always after being exalted over God.

> *But you said in your heart, "I will ascend to heaven; I will raise my throne above the stars of God, and I will sit on the mount of assembly in the recesses of the north. I will ascend above the heights of the clouds; I will make myself like the Most High." Nevertheless you will be thrust down to Sheol, to the recess of the pit* (Isaiah 14:13-15).

Our attention belongs to God! It's Him we focus our worship and adoration on. Not the problems, not the chaos, not injustice even—but on Him. The cry of the warrior is, "I worship You, even now, even right now. I worship *You*. I turn my eyes to You; may they be fixed on You. Let nothing distract my focus; my attention belongs to You. I worship You, even right now in the middle of it all. You alone are worthy. You deserve my praise. I stop and set my mind on worshiping you."

It's hard. Even in the midst of pain or busyness, the warrior Bride always creates space to worship and adore Jesus through it all. Worship isn't just about giving Jesus our best during church on Sunday. *No*—I believe it's about praising God through the mound of dishes; through the tears of hurt, pain, and loss; through the valleys and the heights and joys of life, too. It's a mindset of, "I'll chose to fix my gaze on Jesus and Him alone."

I just invite you right now to join me in a moment of getting really still in our thoughts and minds. Let's take this moment of our day to invite God in to speak to our hearts.

> *Lord, would You reveal if there is any area that we are focusing our attention on instead of You? Is there anything distracting me? You deserve to be first. Would You bring us back to that place of the first time we fell in love with You? Bring us back to intimacy and let nothing bring separation between us. Amen.*

As we choose worship, our focus shifts off our problems. It shifts our focus off of what the enemy is doing and puts it on God. What we behold we become more like. God is our Jehovah Nissi, our Banner, and He fights our battles for us (see Exod. 17).

In the vision of the warrior Bride and the battlefield shared at the beginning of this book, I heard God's voice saying, "Shift your focus. We are winning! Find the beat of My heart." The ability to turn our eyes away from ourselves and place them on Jesus is one of the greatest weapons we may have in times of war.

When It All Goes Wrong

But what about when life doesn't work out the way we planned or wanted it to? What then? "Where was God when…"—I'm sure we can all fill in the blank.

Here is my friend Jenny Weaver's story of dealing with the loss of their son and how praise pulled them through it.

> I remember saying, "Praise is my weapon" many times before I ever realized just exactly what it meant.
>
> I know how it feels to have people say to you in the midst of a storm, "Praise your way out," and you nod and agree and say amen but still have no clue how you can actually do that.
>
> My full testimony is full of miracles and it's just an amazing story of God taking me from a suicidal, self-cutting, homeless drug addict who practiced witchcraft and lived an alternative lifestyle to being a whole and healed mom, wife, traveling worship leader, recording artist, and published author! I give God all the praise because He truly is a good Father.
>
> Part of my testimony began in the early summer of 2017. My husband and I were trying to have a baby for several years so our seven-year-old daughter could have a little brother or sister.
>
> One day I felt that maybe I was pregnant, but after many negative pregnancy tests I didn't want to get

my hopes up. But this time felt different, so while on our family vacation I went off to get a test. I couldn't believe it said positive, so I took another one to be sure and both said pregnant! I told my husband and we both were so excited about this new child.

To shorten a long story of many ups and downs with our faith and hopes, my husband and I ended up losing that baby. If that weren't devastating enough, it was a rare occurrence. It was a molar pregnancy and basically the fetus had turned into a tumor-like mass and I would now have to see a special doctor and possibly have to get radiation treatments.

Right then and there in that hospital room after shedding tears and holding my husband, I under-stood the meaning of *praise is my weapon*. I said out loud, "God, we give You praise. I don't have the answers right now, but we give You glory, we give you praise, we do not blame You, we do not question You. We say that You are good; You're good, Father." That following Sunday, I was scheduled to lead worship. When my pastor told me that I didn't have to worry about leading worship that Sunday, I responded to him that I most definitely would be leading worship that Sunday and that I genuinely wanted to. That morning I got on the platform and the first words out of my mouth were, "Hallelujah, God is good and we've come to praise His name!"

That was a defining moment for me when I truly understood the phrase *praise is my weapon*. Although I had been saying it for years, until you're walking through a storm you truly don't understand what that means, and I was able to praise my way out of that situation. A few months after that my ministry took off and my influence grew tremendously and I believe it was a direct result of giving God praise in all circumstances.

God's heart does not want us to suffer and go through pain, but what we do when we are going through it, is truly the measure of our relationship with Him. Sacrificial worship says, "Even when I don't understand, God, how You are working this for good, I will still praise You." Our love and adoration is not based on what we get from God but on who He is. Our love dance is not just looking to God for solutions (although we want them!) but simply saying, "I love You, Father," and He responds back, "I love you more." I am convinced our raw adoration, no matter what season of life we are facing, moves Heaven.

Chapter 4

The Dance of Breaking Chains and Deliverance

We are triune beings—body, spirit, and soul. What we feed each of these and how we take care of them is so critical. God cares about each part as well. We can see that throughout Scripture.

> *Or do you not know that your body is a temple of the Holy Spirit who is in you, whom you have from God, and that you are not your own? For you have been bought with a price: therefore glorify God in your body* (1 Corinthians 6:19-20).

> *Only give heed to yourself and keep your soul diligently* (Deuteronomy 4:9).

Examine me, O Lord, and try me; test my mind and my heart (Psalm 26:2).

Incline your ear and hear the words of the wise, and apply your mind to my knowledge (Proverbs 22:17).

And He said to him, "You shall love the Lord your God with all your heart, and with all your soul, and with all your mind" (Matthew 22:37).

We are destroying speculations and every lofty thing raised up against the knowledge of God, and we are taking every thought captive to the obedience of Christ (2 Corinthians 10:5).

Before we move on here to discuss breaking chains and deliverance, it's important right now for us to stop and ask Holy Spirit if we could be taking better care of any three of these areas—our body, spirit, or soul. The main area of the soul that I wish to address is one of the largest battlefields I believe the enemy tries to attack us at—our mind. Just this week I was convicted by the Lord of thoughts that I had allowed to dwell in that spot between my ears—my mind—that were not His. "Ana," Jesus said, "what are you saying about yourself and thinking about in this season right now? What am I saying? Do those match up?" Uh oh! Just like that I was convicted and led to match up my thoughts with Christ's. It's a great check, and I highly recommend you and I do that on a regular basis. Stop and ask yourself that question right now. What are you saying about yourself and thinking about in this season right now? Does it match what God is saying? Let's make every effort to change our thoughts to match the thoughts of Christ.

Your Body Is Important

Now, I'll be first to admit that I am no expert on body care, but I do know one thing. When my body feels healthy, my mind feels healthy as well and alert, and my soul is generally healthy too. Because the three are so connected, we cannot overlook the importance of taking care of our body and doing regular maintenance. What we feed our body and put into it is important. Why? If I love my body as God does, I would want to take care of it and value it the way God does. And if I highly value it, then I would want to feed it the best. Whew! Even as I'm writing this I'm getting convicted to cut back on the caffeine and ingest more greens.

Do you ever feel like it is so easy to maintain the other two—to focus on keeping your spirit and soul healthy (taking all our thoughts captive)—but overlook the importance of taking care of your body? Currently, I am in a season when life is so busy! Any given week, I find myself doing the regular blessings of laundry, dishes, and cleaning the house that I can never keep clean with children of ages six and under. Besides that, right now we are in the middle of a total house renovation, so I am finding myself using all kinds of skill sets I never had before—such as ripping up tile for hours upon hours. (House renovation is not for sissies!) On top of that, my own traveling ministry keeps me busy, directing weekly healing rooms, and homeschooling my children. The list seems to go on and on.

So here I find myself in this busy season of life, placing high value on spending time with Jesus, getting in the Word of God—feeding my soul! One day, I was sitting with my Bible wide open talking to God, and I heard Him whisper something to me: "Your body is important to Me too, Ana! How are you taking care of it in this season? You need to value rest." Just then, I was super convicted of the way I had been drilling my body into the ground, not getting much sleep, pushing and pushing to get ahead of my schedule; meanwhile, my body was suffering. "Take care of yourself," I heard Him say.

Can you relate? Before I move on, would you do me a favor? Would you be willing to say a prayer with me if the area of your body is an area that you know you're not taking great care of?

> *Jesus, thank You for this body and the way You made it. I appreciate it, even though it may not be perfect. I thank You and declare good health for myself and a good functioning temple. Father, show me now if there is any way I need to be taking care of it better. Amen.*

Now right as I finished praying that with you, I sensed from the Holy Spirit that some of us (myself included) need to hit the reset button with our bodies. God has already given you the instructions on how to get it in shape and how to take care of your body better with healthy foods. But some of us are just so tired in this season and feel discouraged even before we begin. Well, today's the day, my friends.

Today's the Day!

I am going to hit that reset button with you and commit myself today to get back into that workout program I know that I need to do to strengthen my posture, and I will drink my greens today. Will you commit to God to hit that reset button with me?

Another thing I was sensing from Holy Spirit as I finished praying is that some of you need to start saying, "I love my body." I heard and saw the phrase, "Self-acceptance is a key." What you are saying about your body out loud or even in your thoughts is important. Why? What we feed our souls and minds often is displayed in our bodies. Lies we believe about ourselves or even negative talk feeds our souls and minds with negativity.

Once I was praying for a lady at a church conference, and as I laid hands on her I saw something I had never seen before. I saw in a vision a picture of her cells, and the cells looked moon-shaped or not whole. When I looked closer at those cells, I saw the word *negativity* written on them. In that moment, the Lord gave me revelation: "Self-criticism is a struggle." I asked her first if I could pray for her healing, then I asked her if self-criticism could be something she sometimes struggles with. She melted in my arms weeping, and I ended up leading her through deliverance of negative thought patterns over her body. Then her healing came. From what I saw, I now believe negativity can actually affect our bodies at a cellular level.

Now, I'll be first to say my body's not perfect. I'm sure every person can pick out something they wish looked different or were improved on about their body. So I'm not talking here about denying that there is room for improvement. What I am saying is that there has to be a way we can talk about our bodies that remains positive and in alignment with how Jesus sees us. So do me a favor if you can relate to that word about needing more self-acceptance. Pray with me this prayer:

> *Thank You, Jesus, for my body. It's not perfect, but I love it. God, You are going to help me take care of this body and love it the way You do. I commit myself to speak over my body in love and catch any negative thoughts I am saying or having about myself. I choose self-acceptance right now, and I repent for times I have cursed my very own body. I speak healing right now over my own body, if I need it, and I bless my body as a beautiful temple of the Holy Spirit. Amen.*

Mind and Soul Be Healed!

Now I want to talk about an area I feel is very important, especially if you are contending for healing or desire to see the sick healed, and that is the area of the soul and mind. As I made reference to before, lies that we are believing often will manifest through our bodies. The devil is the chief of liars, and he is often so strategic in how he tries to attack us.

> *Whenever he speaks a lie, he speaks from his own nature, for he is a liar and the father of lies* (John 8:44).

Often people will contact me (because I am a seer) and ask me if I see if some witch somewhere has placed a curse on them. More often than not the answer is *no!* We can think the enemy is somewhere outside of ourselves when really we are often our greatest enemy. Where the enemy attacks us the most is through our own thought life—through our mind.

If I have hooked into a lie, then my perspective is tainted. I'm not seeing with a clear vision. As we hook into lies we believe about ourselves, our circumstances, or others, we are opening a door to the enemy as if saying, "I believe what you say is true, so here's a door of access for you."

Wait. Stop and read that again. That is key for all of us in breaking the chains of the enemy.

> *So Jesus said to them again, "Truly, truly, I say to you,*
> *I am the door of the sheep"* (John 10:7).

Doors and gates are referred to many times in the Bible. What you allow into the gate of your mind and your soul will directly correlate to how much freedom, victory, and authority you will carry.

Deliverance from Lies

Here's a little something I do on a regular basis. I get still with the Lord and quiet my mind so that no distracting thoughts are there. Then I ask the Lord, "Are there any lies I currently believe that are not of You? Would You show me?" And then I wait. Just last week, I heard a response from the Lord when I asked that question: "You are believing that you can't handle this. That it's too much for you. That's not truth, Ana. You can do this. You were made for this."

Upon doing this little daily check, if God whispers something to you that is a lie you are believing, here's what I would do with it. Repent for it. Confess it to a friend or pastor you trust so they can keep you accountable and help you walk in freedom from the lifestyle associated with that lie. Then find as many resources as you can that minister to this specific area, if you need more ministry.

Replace with Truth

Next, it is important to ask the Lord to fill you with the truth about that situation. Now, even if you don't believe the truth you hear from the Lord at first, start claiming it and declaring it over yourself. Say it out loud daily if you have to, and watch as it will change from unbelief to belief and then eventually to reality. Finding scriptures to declare over yourself that go along with that truth helps and edifies you immensely.

Just this week, as I faced countless tasks and began to feel overwhelmed, I kept reminding myself, "I can handle this. I was made for this. I can do all things through Christ who strengthens me. Philippians 4:13!" Each time I would say it, it's like a huge weight was lifted off my shoulder, and I felt encouraged to just keep pressing ahead. Speaking the truth the Lord had shared with me and then applying the Word of God to back up that truth released strength that was beyond my own.

> *I will give you the keys of heaven's kingdom realm to forbid on earth that which is forbidden in heaven, and to release on earth that which is released in heaven* (Matthew 16:19 TPT).

> *And do not be conformed to this world, but be transformed by the renewing of your mind, so that you may prove what the will of God is, that which is good and acceptable and perfect* (Romans 12:2).

These two scriptures are reason enough to not allow the enemy to gain any ground in that space between our ears. The word *forbid* here is so much stronger than just "I don't want to agree with the enemy's lies." No—I *forbid* them to take up space and dwell in my mind.

I forbid them to take up space and dwell in my mind!

I want to take every thought captive by daily renewing my mind through the Word of God and by agreeing with what He says. As I agree with that truth, I am releasing on earth that which has already been promised in Heaven.

There is so much power in doing daily declarations. Have you started making daily declarations over yourself and your family using the Word of God? The Word of God is active and sharper than a two-edged sword. As you release it over yourself, you are taking ground against the enemy of this world. You are shifting the spiritual atmosphere around yourself and causing the enemy to retreat when you apply the Word of God to your life.

When I started to dig through Scripture to find some golden nuggets to apply to my life, at first it felt overwhelming. *Lord, where do I start?* I thought.

If you need a good place to start, I highly recommend Patricia King's book *Decrees*. It's one of those books that I like to read out loud on a daily basis.

Let's stop and do a little exercise. How do you feel about yourself? Really, how do you? There is no shame in being honest here. Take a moment and honestly answer that question. This is just between you and God. If you are struggling to answer that question with an answer that matches how God sees you, you may find yourself in a place of needing a transformation in your mindset.

Fill in the blank with me here with a truth that God says about you: "I am _____."

Now do a few more just for fun. It's a great way to kick-start your day.

Prayer

> God, I pray blessing over our minds. Help us to take every thought captive and only believe and speak over ourselves what You are saying. Renew our minds today. Amen.

Spotting Your Enemy

Have you ever felt like there is major oppression going on in your life and the enemy seems to have a bull's-eye marked on your back? I believe that spotting your enemy is a huge key in combatting him.

Let me explain. Many times as I find myself praying for people, the Lord will open my spiritual eyes as a seer to see where the enemy has an access point to attack them. I'll see words over people's bodies such as "unforgiveness, rejection, self-hatred" etc., or other times I'll see areas of people's bodies highlighted and it will be a good indication for me of what needs healing so I can pray. It's not like that every time, but sometimes it is. By seeing where the enemy is attacking, I'll know how to combat him in prayer.

I personally have walked through this many times. One time I was to be filmed on a major television show with Marilyn Hickey and Sarah Bowling. I arrived to my hotel the day before and tried to enter into prayer mode. I thought, *If ever there was a time I needed to hear from You, God, now would be a good time right before I am about to go on this huge show and reach so many people sitting at home through media.*

As I began to try and pray in my room, it was like something was literally blocking my ears entirely from being able to hear the voice of God. I sat for hours trying everything I knew to do. I prayed, I worshiped, I read Scripture out loud, I got real still to listen to God—and *nothing.* Frustrated, I said out loud, "Come on, God. Where are You? I need to hear from You!" Then I heard just one thing from the Lord: "Something is in the room. Spot your enemy."

That's when I realized that there was literally a spirit or some sort of attack assigned to me to block me from being able to hear the voice of God. Like a wall put up, it was hindering me from being able to climb up and ascend to meet with Jesus.

"Lord, would You open my spiritual eyes to see what is in the room here? Show me what has been assigned against me," I prayed.

Just then I saw on the wall of the hotel room the phrase *fear of man.* For me this was a first-time experience where I was allowed to see what was residing in my hotel room before I got there. Now, I can't tell you why it was there or what had happened with the previous person who stayed in the room. I can only share with you that once I knew what I was up against—an actual spirit that was in the room—I knew how to combat it.

I began to pray and instantly thank the Lord that He has not given me a spirit of fear but of power, love, and a sound mind (see 2 Tim. 1:7). I asked the Lord to reveal to me if there was any area in my life where I was carrying fear or had made an agreement with fear. He revealed a few things, and I immediately renounced them or prayed to break my agreement with them. Once I had gotten rid of any fear areas I had been walking in, I commanded that spirit of fear to leave my room and stop hindering me from hearing the voice of God.

In Daniel 10:13 the angel Michael is seen combating a principality.

> *But the prince of the kingdom of Persia was withstanding me for twenty-one days; then behold, Michael, one of the chief princes, came to help me, for I had been left there with the kings of Persia.*

It's good to take a look at this because realistically sometimes we are truly up against something in the spirit that needs to be broken off. I never go around looking for demons to go up against. I don't need to. I see them. Truth be told, our job is to focus and set our adoration on our King Jesus. But when something like a principality is blocking us from being able to maintain that place of intimacy, it needs to be stripped down.

Back to my story. That spirit did not go right away. I share this to encourage many of you who know you are up against something, but there is a little bit of a struggle for it to leave. There are principalities that I have prayed and commanded to leave that go instantly, and then there are others that take a little more work to get to leave. Perhaps this is why Jesus said, *"But this kind does not go out except by prayer and fasting"* (Matt. 17:21). It gives us hope to keep standing on the Word, and eventually that principality will leave. Keep going, beloved. Don't give up!

After commanding it to leave, I could still sense the spirit in the room. I quoted a few more scriptures and then began to worship. Worship always sets the atmosphere for spirits to flee. I'll be the first to admit that I'm not the best singer, but *man* let me tell you—when I'm up against something, suddenly my voice becomes a whole lot stronger! I worshiped and worshiped, and the Presence of God filled the room. The spirit left, and then Jesus walked into the room!

Then Jesus walked into the room!

Did you catch that? I was on the floor worshiping and suddenly looked up and saw my precious Jesus walk right into the room. I then had the sweetest encounter with the Lord, and boy, was I prepared with a message for that television show the next day!

Why Spotting Your Enemy Is Key

I believe many of us struggle with knowing how the enemy is actually attacking us. Yes, we may have the symptoms, such as a disease manifesting in our body, anxiety, depression, etc.

But how that disease had access to stick there—that is the real question. *If* the enemy has gained an access point, once we gain understanding it's easier to defeat him. In the story mentioned above, I was actually coming up against an atmospheric demon, so not all attacks of the enemy are due to our own sin issues.

Overseas, my husband and I experienced this many times. I'll never forget when we went to Varanasi, India where there was so much demonic activity. Temples are everywhere there; there is still human trafficking there; and animals are still slaughtered and offered to idols and Hindu gods. We went there to just prayer walk around the city. As soon as we got there, I could barely walk within 100 feet of the temple areas without becoming super sick. I felt instant nausea and had to sit with my head between my knees to keep myself from vomiting everywhere.

This was a wonderful lesson for us! *Don't* take on demons and principalities unless you have a clear word of the Lord to do so. While it was a wonderful idea to go walk and pray around the city, the Lord hadn't instructed us to do that. I have seen many people get hurt and very sick after taking on a demonic principality that had a real stronghold in an area, and they immaturely (as I had done) stepped up to take on something they were not assigned by the Lord to do. Let me be clear—I am in no way moving in fear of the enemy, for I know whom I serve and the power of Christ is within me. But I want to do as Jesus did and *only* do as the Father says. When we try to operate out of our own strength, without a clear command of the Lord, this is when we dangerously step out from under our covering.

I repeat, *not all attacks of the enemy are due to our own sin issues.* The reason I say this is because there are so many people suffering in this world. We can't walk around and start preaching a message of "you are sick because you did this." That is absolutely lacking compassion. Rather, let's go to prayer and ask the Lord to reveal where the enemy is attacking. Let's ask the Lord to reveal strategies in how to pray. Let's also ask Him if there is any inner lie we have believed that is giving the enemy permission to reside. Imagine a snake that is lurking around, searching for a place to hook his fangs into. He sees a lie being believed: "My husband doesn't really love me," or, "I'm never going to be like that. I'm just not good enough compared to that person," etc. Then that snake hooks into the lies that sometimes infiltrate our mind and breaths into them. He feeds the lie, and as we believe it to be true our bodies and emotions respond.

So catching and spotting the enemy's attacks is a key in stopping him in his tracks and not allowing him to continue. *Not on my watch!* Get behind me, satan!

Combat Time: Overcoming Witchcraft

Not every attack is from a witch sitting somewhere in her house, stirring her pot of dark magic. Most of the time the greatest attack we face from the enemy as believers is in the battle of our mind. The enemy is a liar and a deceiver, and often he tries to whisper lies to us and get us to believe those lies about ourselves.

However, there are times when there are real witchcraft assignments or curses released onto us. Like fiery arrows, witchcraft is meant to silence us warriors, steal our voice, attack our health, and sometimes hit those closest to us to make us weary. I want to share a personal story here of when witchcraft became real to me. I had an eye-opening experience that to this day makes me fiery about teaching others how to combat spiritual warfare, specifically when witchcraft is involved. Patricia King has a book, *Exposed: Witchcraft in the Church*, that I highly recommend if you want to go further into studying this. Derek Prince also has much helpful material.

A Wake-up Call

For me, this was a real wake-up call to spiritual warfare, demonic presences, and witchcraft. My husband and I had just come from Mozambique, Africa with Heidi and Rolland Baker and found ourselves in Kolkata, India. We went there with the intention to pioneer a ministry. Experiencing spiritual warfare was not new to us, as we had been with the Bakers in Mozambique. Witch doctors there tried to place curses on our team all the time. But Jesus is *victorious!* Hallelujah!

That being said, within the first week we arrived my husband became violently sick. I found myself in a country whose language I didn't understand. I didn't feel the safest where we were staying (a local hostel). Only my husband could read the signs, as he had previously been to India as a missionary for two years and speaks Bengali. But there he was, unconscious and dehydrated from being violently sick. Days went by where he couldn't hold any food or water down. I wasn't even sure where to find a good hospital, so I really had no idea what to do. We also did not have working cell phones, and I didn't know how to use internet cafés yet.

Looking at my husband groaning on the bed, passing in and out of consciousness, I cried out to God. "God, what should I do? I'm alone in this. Please help me, Lord."

"Go to the bathroom," I heard the Lord respond. "See what is there." Apprehensively, I went down to the hallway communal bathroom. The Holy Spirit led me to open one stall and look.

To my surprise, I opened the stall and found a Sadhu priest sitting there. He held a picture of my husband and was doing chants and throwing ashes and flowers in the air.

From what I know from being a missionary overseas, Sadhu priests are Hindu priests and fortune-tellers in India. While in India, I saw many tourists seeking "religious experiences" go to Sadhu priests and be prayed over or blessed. Little did they realize what they were truly opening themselves up to in the spiritual realm!

When I saw him, righteous anger rose up in me. "You have no authority or power to be messing with my husband. We are covered and bought with the blood of the Lamb! Now it is time for you to go! Your deal here is *done* in Jesus' name!" And just like that—*poof!* He disappeared.

Now, I've heard some Christians mention being transported or moved in location, and we can even see that biblically (see Luke 24:36), but this was my first time seeing a witch doctor transported. There's always a counterfeit!

I went back to check on my husband and found him now sitting up in bed, saying he was hungry. Praise God!

Witchcraft is real, and I believe the church needs a wake-up call. It's not that we need to fear the demonic, as we have been paid for with the blood of Jesus Christ. But to think that it is essentially non-existent is obliviousness. It is time for us to rise up and step into the authority Jesus has paid for.

Generational Curses and Patterns

One key that I have found in spotting the enemy is that sometimes we may be up against a generational curse or pattern that we don't even realize exists. I distinctly remember working with a young woman once who shared with me that she had struggled with worry and fear her entire life. No matter how many inner healing sessions, counseling, and healing prayer models she had tried (all of which I totally believe are good things to do), this still continued to rise up and be a real battle for her.

I instantly went to prayer and asked the Lord to show me where fear and anxiety had first entered her or come over her. With my eyes closed, I saw a distinct prophetic picture of three women who had similar physical traits. The third was full-term pregnant.

After getting some direction from the Holy Spirit, I said, "I believe what you are truly up against here is a generational curse of fear and anxiety that came from your mother's side. I see three generations of women and you in your mother's womb being the fourth carrying this curse." As I said this, she began to wail and cry out with an unearthly scream. She hit the floor flailing and crying. I knelt down beside her calmly and said, "In Jesus' name, I declare that the blood of Jesus is enough to break the generational curse *now* of fear and anxiety. Fear and anxiety *go!*" As I did this, the lady gave a final scream and then instantly calmed down. Her body went limp like she was exhausted, and then the sweet, peaceful Presence of the Lord came into the room and renewed her. After some time, I helped her get up off the floor and sit back down. "How are you feeling now? What do you feel?" I asked.

"Peace!" she said. "So peaceful! Wow!"

My Own Deliverance Testimony

Now I want to share my own personal deliverance story, as I know this subject of deliverance often can scare many people or seem a bit bizarre to say the least. I start off this story by posing a question: "Can a Christian be delivered of a demonic attack?" Many people have different views on this very subject, and it can be a bit controversial. Let's go there!

Here's my story. I was in my mid-20s and a student at the International House of Prayer University. I was a Christian and had been around many swirls of the Holy Spirit growing up, as my mom works in inner-healing ministry, and I also had been a missionary in many different countries since the age of fourteen. I was fresh out of the mission field of Brazil, where my seer anointing had been really opened to see not only angelic activity and heavenly encounters with Jesus, but also demonic activity in the streets of Brazil. (My first book, *The Seer's Path,* shares this story in more detail.)

So there I was in a Bible study meeting one night. A couple who were known to move in the deliverance and healing power of the Lord came to teach our little group. I remember them starting to pray, and if I am being completely honest, I had the prideful thought: *I don't need any deliverance! I have been through so much inner healing—sozo, theophostics, counseling—you name it, I've done it.*

Not the best open mentality I had going into this meeting, I'll admit! The gentleman looked at me and gently but firmly said, "Freemasonry in your bloodline." The next thing that happened was beyond my control. I remember that I was tossed off my chair and knocked straight forward onto the floor. I felt a weird vibration that was a bit scary at first going through my body as he gently knelt down beside me and began to pray. The gentle but firm way he prayed and led me through deliverance was beautiful!

On a side note, deliverance does not always need to look like what old movies depict—the yelling, "thumping over the head with a Bible" type preaching—although I have seen this to be effective sometimes as well. Deliverance can be calm, gentle, and yet with complete authority and the power of Jesus to kick that curse and demon right out!

He prayed out loud that he felt like the Lord had showed him that I carried the witchcraft of masonry somewhere down my bloodline and that the Lord wanted to set me free of that tonight. What was crazy about this whole thing was that I had just recently discovered through my mom's research that we did, in fact, carry freemasonry in our bloodline. He prayed for that curse to be broken and lifted off by the blood of the Lamb, and I kid you not—I felt something lift off of me, and I felt physically lighter after that prayer time.

Now that kind of thing you just can't make up, and why would I even want to?

Now that kind of thing you just can't make up!

That day, the Lord brought real deliverance from a curse that had been on my own generational lineage, and it was just so beautiful. Deliverance from curses does not need to be something scary or unapproachable in the church. It shouldn't be!

I recently ran into an acquaintance outside of a coffee shop. She talked to me about reoccurring fears and demonic attacks that she keeps getting hit with. "I keep asking the Lord to reveal to me if there are any doors I've opened, any sin issues I may have that are giving the enemy permission to keep attacking me...but I just keep getting nothing." Right away, as I was standing there listening, I saw the words *generational curse* written across her forehead.

While I will be first to admit that I don't fully understand generational curses, I know they are real just from experience. I have seen hundreds delivered of curses and be instantly healed, set free, and transformationally renewed. What I share is perhaps just the tip of the iceberg as a whole book could be written on this one topic. Please see the works of Marilyn Hickey and Peter and Doris Wagner if you wish to study this subject more in-depth.

As a seer (which you can dive further into in my first book *The Seer's Path*), the Lord will often speak to me by opening my spiritual eyes to show me pictures or give me words of direction or knowledge through seeing prophetically. The term *seer* is completely biblical (see 1 Sam. 9:11; 2 Sam. 24:11; 1 Chron. 9:22; 21:9; 2 Chron. 19:2; 29:25; 33:18—just in case you were curious). There are many more examples you can look up.

I share these stories here because perhaps you yourself are experiencing something similar. No matter how pure you are trying to keeping your life, there seems to be a sticking place of attack that the enemy hits you at. You may be up against a generational curse or pattern. Do you find yourself constantly struggling with the same stronghold again and again? No matter what you do to try and get free, there it comes back again? Let's take a moment and not move on too quickly.

Let's ask Holy Spirit to reveal, right now, if there perhaps is a generational curse, pattern, or stronghold that may be operating here in your life today.

Here are a few generational curses or patterns that I have led people through deliverance from. There are so many, but here are a few larger roots that I see most often:

- Substance addictions
- Self-pity
- Orphan spirit
- Pride
- Control
- Jealousy
- Sexual lust

- Spirit of poverty

- Freemasonry

- Self-hatred

- "I'm not good enough" mentality

- Fatalism

- Spirit of performance

- Insecurity

- Rejection

- Fear

- Victim spirit

- Witchcraft

- Physical iniquities

Many diseases are generational curses. For example—diabetes, cancer, eyesight problems, heart problems, respiratory issues, reproductive issues such as menstruation problems, ovarian or uterus problems, kidney problems, etc. There are many others, but these are just a few larger ones that come up most frequently in prayer for people.

Prayer for Breaking Free from a Generational Curse

If Holy Spirit is highlighting something to you right now, here is a simple but powerful prayer I do with people to break the chains of that generational curse.

> *In Jesus' name, right now, I recognize that there is a generational curse of _____ on my family and I repent for it. I break the generational*

curse of _____ off of myself and my bloodline. I plead the blood of Jesus Christ over myself and my bloodline and declare that by His stripes I am set free. One drop of Your blood, Jesus, was enough. I bind the enemy from attacking me or my family line with this curse anymore. I thank You, Lord, that now I am free from _____, and today I choose _____ instead. Amen.

It is really important that you do that last bit. You are choosing to fill your spirit with truths and blessings from Jesus instead of the lie the enemy has fed you. You are reversing the curse into the blessing of the Lord!

You may be reading this and thinking, *Now hold up. Why do I have to cleanse my bloodline if I have Jesus Christ within me? Doesn't the truth "Whom the son sets free is free indeed" mean anything?* Marilyn Hickey writes:

> The blood of Jesus is all sufficient, powerful, and devastating to family iniquities in your bloodline. To be effective, however, the blood of Jesus must be applied to your situation.[1]

The truth is, anytime there is a curse, there must be blood shed to break and reverse the curse. For this reason, how wonderful is it that we can claim freedom from all curses by applying to our bloodline the blood that Jesus Christ bled for us!

We all carry family patterns and tendencies, whether those be a curse or a blessing. I can see this every day when I look at my daughter, who is now six. With hands on her hips, she'll say something to her little brother that I know is my voice speaking right through her to him! "You have to wipe up your water from your sippy cup if you spill it everywhere, buddy!" she'll say. *Oh boy*, I think. *She's picking up my little sayings and tendencies like a sponge!* It's important we think about and value the legacy that we pass on to our children. Or when I go to the doctor for my regular checkup, they ask me a series of questions about the history of the health of previous family members. Although they are way down the lineage, doctors still want to know. They wouldn't use these same terms, but in truth they believe in this whole curse thing—generational iniquity and sins that can be passed down even four generations.

> *Who keeps lovingkindness for thousands, who forgives iniquity, transgression and sin; yet He will by no means leave the guilty unpunished, visiting the iniquity of fathers on the children and on the grandchildren to the third and fourth generations* (Exodus 34:7).

We Don't Need to Live on the Defense

Praise God that through the power of Jesus Christ we can walk in freedom and the fullness He has for us! It's important that we do as the Bible says and only do what we see the Father doing (see John 5:19). Holy Spirit is good and will only bring up what needs to be addressed. We don't need to live on the defense, constantly looking at our past or generational lineage and asking the Lord continually to cleanse it. He is good. He will bring up anything that needs to be addressed, and we can rest and trust God in that and set our focus more on what the Lord is doing than the attacks of the enemy. So don't keep looking back down your generational lineage unless the Lord leads you to it.

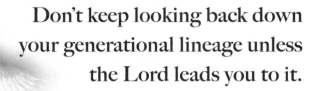

Don't keep looking back down your generational lineage unless the Lord leads you to it.

It's important with generational curses and blessing that we don't walk around continually looking at our lineage out of a place of fear that we left some stones unturned. Jesus wants you and I to walk in absolute freedom with Him *today!* He is good and will guide you.

Backdoor Creepers

With a section title like that, you may think, *What is she talking about?* I want to take a look at two familiar scriptures that reveal demonic activity.

> *When the unclean spirit goes out of a man, it passes through waterless places seeking rest, and not finding any, it says, "I will return to my house from which I came." And when it comes, it finds it swept and put in order* (Luke 11:24-25).

> *When He came to the other side into the country of the Gadarenes, two men who were demon-possessed met Him as they were coming out of the tombs. They were so extremely violent that no one could pass by that*

way. And they cried out, saying, "What business do we have with each other, Son of God? Have You come here to torment us before the time?" Now there was a herd of many swine feeding at a distance from them. The demons began to entreat Him, saying, "If You are going to cast us out, send us into the herd of swine." And He said to them, "Go!" And they came out and went into the swine, and the whole herd rushed down the steep bank into the sea and perished in the waters (Matthew 8:28-32).

These two scriptures shed an interesting light on demonic activities or strategies.

#1 Demons often will try to return to previous attacks.

I have personally seen and experienced this myself. Have you ever experienced this yourself? Perhaps you go to a prayer meeting, receive prayer for healing, and get touched by the Lord, only to have that previous pain return a few days later? Or perhaps you get set free from a real deep fear that you carried, and then just following that freedom the enemy attacks you with something that in the natural would stir up fear in you again.

There is a strategy the enemy uses here. He cannot create as God; the devil is a liar and tries old ways to weaken us.

As I shared earlier, growing up I had lots of throat problems. Many infections, tonsillitis, strep throat, and loss of my voice. This continued most of my life, until one day when I was in Mozambique with Heidi and Rolland Baker, I heard Holy Spirit whisper, "Ask Me what the root of this is!" I took it to prayer, and immediately I saw a clear vision from the Lord of memories as a child and other times as an adult when I felt like I couldn't speak up and so suppressed my own voice and opinion from being heard. I walked through repentance for this and also received some wonderful inner healing from the Lord. I broke agreement with old lies that Holy Spirit uncovered, lies I believed about myself, my own voice, and also my interaction with others, and I asked the Lord to replace those with truths. As I came into agreement with those truths—which took some time of really declaring them over myself until I could actually believe what I was saying—my throat was completely healed.

Now fast-forward to a few years later. As I was preparing for ministry, an old familiar pain came back on my right tonsil. My throat began to tighten as it had previously done for all those years of my life, and my voice gave out instantly.

No. This can't be happening! I thought to myself.

"You have victory over this, Ana," I heard Holy Spirit say. "You cast it out and it will go!"

So I did just that. I laid hands on my own throat and commanded that ugly spirit that was trying to paralyze and oppress my voice again to go. I claimed the blood of the Lamb over myself, and immediately my throat opened and my voice returned.

What you have victory in, you can reclaim and hold your ground!

What you have victory in, you can then reclaim and hold your ground. The enemy may try to return in that same old way, but you can have victory! Remind yourself and the Lord of your testimony of being healed or set free of that in the past and watch that attack go.

Right now, take a moment to pause and ask Holy Spirit to reveal if there is any area in your life where you once had victory and overcame, but you are now being attacked in again. I encourage you to claim and declare over yourself:

> *I have had victory in _____ area, and I declare that I am free of this. No longer can I be afflicted or mentally tortured in this area again. I command _____ to go right now by the blood of the Lamb. By His stripes I have been healed!*

This goes without saying, but I better add it in here. Make sure your "house is swept clean"—meaning make sure there is no sin area in your life that would open the door for the enemy to attack you again. If Holy Spirit now reveals anything to you that you need to get right with Jesus on, simply pray and repent for it, and turn away from it. This brings me to my next point.

#2 Demons need somewhere to land, so don't become a landing ground.

I'll never forget this eye-opening experience my husband and I had when ministering in Nepal. We were in the heart of Kathmandu, thick with Hindu temples and idol worship. As we walked the streets lined with sickening idols and witchcraft trinkets for sale, the ministry team we were a part of decided it was a good location to ask Jesus to do some miracles. People were so open to receive prayer for healing there. (Jesus was just another "god" to the Hindus as they worship like 4 million gods.)

Our team sat down with a man who at first seemed so angry. When we prayed for him, his back was completely healed, and then he received his eyesight back. I'll never forget the look in his face and countenance change. After he got his miracle, right there he accepted Jesus into his heart. A crowd pressed in around us as they wanted to see what all the commotion was about. After he accepted the Lord, I witnessed the weirdest occurrence. The crowd around us rose up against us angrily, ready to harm us. Our translator, who was also a part of our ministry team, quickly saved us and got us out of there. As we turned to leave, he said to me, "See, the angry spirit that was in that man jumped onto the crowd." Wow! That scripture about the demons asking to go into the pigs has come alive to me all the more now.

Do everything you can to make sure you are not a landing ground for any demonic activity. Take a moment right now and ask the Lord to reveal to you if there is anything in your own heart that isn't pure before His sight. Often, for Christians, the message of repentance isn't preached as much now, but it is so valuable and so much a part of the Gospel that we can't overlook it. If you find something as you do this heart check that doesn't line up with the nature of Christ—which is full of peace, love, joy, compassion, understanding, grace, forgiveness, etc.—repent and ask the Lord to forgive you and wash you clean.

Jesus came that we may have abundant life and the likeness of His image.

Feeding Our Emotions

What's feeding your emotions right now? I mean it. Really stop and do a heart check. What I believe, is that this warrior Bride that I saw and shared at the opening of the book, is so infused and grounded in the Lord that all of her emotions line up with God's as well. Often, I have to do a heart check. "What's feeding my emotions right now?" This side of Heaven, it's easy to get hit with stuff of the flesh—small offenses, bitterness, irritations, complaints, etc. Let's focus our emotions on Him right now. He's so beautiful and lovely. Here's a simple prayer I find myself praying often when the enemy tries to hook my emotions:

> *God, thank You for a new day, a beautiful reset for my emotions, spirit, and soul. Father, would You refresh me? I set my eyes on You. Thank You for Your love. I am so grateful. I choose peace, love, kindness, forgiveness, goodness, gentleness, hope, encouragement, faith, and self-control. I want to leak Your Presence and glory to those around me. Give me Your heart for others and Your eyes to see from a heavenly perspective. Amen.*

While it is so easy to let our mouths run when we get hit by irritants or even hard attacks of the enemy, I encourage you to keep a muzzle over your mouth. Let not your mouth become a vocal piece for the enemy to release his weapons and fiery darts over you and others. Proverbs 18:21 says, *"Death and life are in the power of the tongue,*" so be careful not to complain. Kingdom-minded people release Kingdom-minded language. God is calling us all up higher to match what He says.

Moving Past the Why and Into the How

Often the tendency when we get hit with the assaults of the enemy is to seek answers as to why this attack occurred. While I do think examination is valuable, it's important not to become fixated on the "why." Listen to this story of a woman who got healed as she stopped looking back.

I had never met anyone quite like this woman. It was a Tuesday evening, and I was there leading one of our healing room teams. Sitting before me was a woman who was so grounded in the Word of God, but hit currently with so much sickness. She had done everything right and done her homework. She had contended for so long for her breakthrough. "Why am I still sick?" she asked me with anger and frustration in her voice. "I've read and spoken the Word over myself every day. I take communion daily. I've asked the Lord to reveal if I've left any open door to the enemy to attack me due to my sin, and I've repented. I worship. I command the sickness to go. But I'm still in pain. I'm still sick. Why?"

The question lingered tensely in the air. What was I to say in response to this woman? What was I to offer as hope? I was filled with compassion for her. *Holy Spirit, help me*, I silently prayed.

Suddenly, the words that could only have been God's came out of my mouth: "I don't know. But it's not okay and God wants you well."

Sighing, I knew this phrase was not going to be sufficient for the lady sitting in front of me. She wanted answers. She wanted reasons as to why she was sick. "I don't know" would just not cut it for her! "Can I pray for you?" I gently asked her.

Looking back at me a little shocked, she shrugged her shoulders. "Sure. Why not!"

I prayed: "Lord, I don't know why she is suffering so much. Only You know what is truly going on here. But I do know that You are the ultimate Healer. Father, I pray that You would heal her now so that she can look forward and not have to keep looking back. I pray she would walk in freedom from this affliction. We love You, Lord, and we choose to set our eyes on You."

Just like that, the Lord's Presence came; she felt warmth all over her body and she was healed.

Now, I still to this day have no idea why God used that moment to heal that woman. Here she had been standing on the Word, declaring, repenting, worshiping for years. But God chose that moment to heal her. Praise God! Hallelujah, He is good!

I share this story in the hope that as we learn to dance the dance of breaking chains and deliverance, we won't get too lost in seeking an answer to the question of *why* we are struggling. It is a fine balance, really. While these are all examples and suggestions to break the chains of the enemy's grip on our lives, it is so valuable and important that we do not keep our eyes and focus fixated there on always trying to figure out the whys and what's causing it. This mindset can lock us into the problem instead of locking us into the solution. God is our answer to how we get set free every time! Let's keep our eyes fixated on our solution—*Jesus.*

Note

1. Marilyn Hickey, *Breaking Generational Curses* (Oklahoma: Harrison House, 2000), 150.

Chapter 5

The Dance of Perspective

"Come up higher, beloved, and see from My view!" How many of us would love to hear that from Jesus sometime? Revelation 3:18 says, *"Purchase eye salve to be placed over your eyes so that you can truly see"* (TPT).

For us to rise to the position of a warrior Bride, we need God's eyes to see with insight. Jesus would always see beyond. He didn't see the impossible and hopeless situation sitting in front of him. "She's just sleeping," He would respond and then call forth a little girl back to life (see Mark 5:39). He wasn't seeing the circumstance in front of Him; He constantly had perspective and wisdom coming directly from the throne room.

One of my most frequent prayers as a seer is, "God, give me eyes to see as You do." And then, He does.

I was just in a meeting in Washington, DC ministering. There I prayed, "God, give me eyes to see the creative miracles You want to release. Lord, don't let me see just what's in front of me. Show me how You see." There I saw a set of brand-new kidneys fall into the room. I don't know how to explain it other than that. As I looked up, I saw a pair of kidneys just fall. I caught them, and then asked who needed a creative miracle of brand-new kidneys. A lady stepped forward who sure enough had major kidney and bladder issues and was facing possible surgery. I laid hands on her and prayed for God to do a creative miracle. Guess what? God did it! The power of God hit that lady who was knocked clear off her feet. As she lay down flat out on her back, she felt all the pain release that had been in her body. Just to test out her creative miracle, she later shared with me that she intentionally went and drank a ton of water, just to see if she could urinate without pain. She was healed! God did it!

Getting God's perspective, is not the same as positive thinking. While I do believe there is some truth in what you put your eyes or focus on, you can have—we want *God's* perspective! God's perspective gives us hope, that what we see happening in the natural is not God's reality.

When He Walks into the Room

When Jesus walks into the room, everything changes. Many of us know this phrase from a very popular worship song, but do we really believe it?

*While He was still speaking, someone came from the house of the synagogue official, saying, "Your daughter has died; do not trouble the Teacher anymore." But when Jesus heard this, He answered him, "Do not be afraid any longer; only believe, and she will be made well." When He came to the house, He did not allow anyone to enter with Him, except Peter and John and James, and the girl's father and mother. Now they were all weeping and lamenting for her; but He said, "Stop weeping, for she has not died, but is asleep." And they began laughing at Him, knowing that she had died. He, **however**, took her by the hand and called, saying, "Child, arise!" And her spirit returned, and she got up immediately; and He gave orders for something to be given her to eat* (Luke 8:49-55).

I love the "however" in this scripture so I just had to add the emphasis! In the natural, things looked pretty grim for this family. Their daughter lay there cold and lifeless. Even the disciples, who were closest to Jesus, laughed at His response. It amazes me, after all the miracles they had seen Jesus perform, that they still did not have faith for this one!

Heaven's Perspective

So, friend, what is Heaven's perspective right now about your current situation? What does God say is the season you are in? Sometimes it is good for us to take a step back from just going through it and ask, "God, what are You doing right now?" Take a moment and literally evaluate what is going on in your life in the natural. What does God say about it?

These are the answers that I want to be proclaiming and declaring over myself and my family. God's answers. God's perspective.

My Testimony of Walking in Faith

I remember when I wrote my first book, *The Seer's Path*. This testimony many do not know, and I pray it will encourage you. When God spoke to me about writing the book, the idea of writing seemed overwhelming to me. Onward I pressed and sat at my computer typing through many sleepless nights, even though I was pregnant with my firstborn. When I completed my book, I heard God tell me clearly "Destiny Image" as a publisher for my book. So I submitted it to them. My book was rejected right away.

Man, did I hear You wrong, God? I thought to myself. I kept praying through that season, holding on to faith, and speaking to that mountain to move. In the meanwhile, other publishing opportunities came along, but none seemed like a right fit. I just didn't have the peace of the Lord to run forward with any of them. Writing a book almost feels like a baby—the hours of sacrifice and prayer you put into it. I couldn't hand my baby over to just anyone! During this time of just waiting and standing in faith on what God had spoken to me, I prayed asking the Lord for strategy.

"God what should I do? I feel like I need to keep moving forward, like You want this to be published, but the right door seems shut," I prayed.

"Walk! Start walking now!" I heard back from the Lord.

Then a crazy idea came to my mind that I know *only* Holy Spirit could have placed there! Only a few months after having given birth to my firstborn child, as a new momma I decided to do a walk-a-thon. I had this crazy idea that I needed to raise money for the project of the book. So I began to train for the big day. Every day I would walk a bit more and more, until finally I was walking on the weekends up to 14 miles, in the middle of the season of poopy diapers and late-night feeding!

The big day came, and I was so excited that I was almost crying as I started to walk. See, to everyone else it seemed like a crazy idea, but I knew I was birthing something in the spirit.

I knew I was birthing something in the spirit.

Long story short, I actually got lost and ended up walking a bit extra—33 miles that day!

I'll never forget that memory, as I came to that finish line limping in pain, and saw my family and friends there waiting to greet me with balloons and cake to celebrate. What I felt in that moment! It brings me to tears just thinking about it now.

"Thank you so much for coming out for this event, friends. I am tired, I am in pain, but I am so happy! Today marks the birthing of my ministry and this day I will *never* forget!" I said to the group there as we celebrated.

Markers and the Tests of Faith

There are seasons in life when God asks us to do things in the natural that I believe unlock things from Heaven or in the supernatural. For me, this walk-a-thon was just that. Every door at the time looked shut. What a wild journey of pushing through discouragement this is. Trust me, I could have walked the easy road and maybe just self-published or gone with a different offer. That thought crossed my mind many times, and each time it rose up I stuck firm with what I had heard. "Nope. Destiny Image is the publisher for me, and God's going to do it somehow."

As I crossed that finish line that day, I heard Heaven's response: "You've been obedient and stood the test of faith. Now watch how I'm going to respond."

Heaven Responds

A few days later, as I was still recovering from the walk (with lots of warm baths, Epsom salts, etc.), something wild and amazing happened. I was doing dishes, looking out my kitchen window, when suddenly I saw an angel walking up my back deck. Do you know what he looked like? I know this might blow your idea of what angels look like (I know it did for me when I saw him!), but let's take a moment and look at what Scripture says about angels.

> *Do not neglect to show hospitality to strangers, for by this some have entertained angels without knowing it* (Hebrews 13:2).

He looked different from any other angel I had ever seen before. He was wearing a black top hat and carrying a black briefcase. He looked at me and stood there waiting. I stopped washing dishes immediately and walked outside to meet him.

"I have a contract from Heaven for you," he said. I watched him open his briefcase and draw out a contract that looked like a scroll. He unrolled it, and in amazement I saw that on the bottom of the page it was signed "God" in gold cursive.

"This is your contract. It comes with a price, though, and it's up to you if you want to sign it." Without hesitation, I signed it immediately. With that he was gone.

A few hours later, Destiny Image called me up on the phone. "We've decided to offer you a contract if you want it. We love your book and would love to publish it," an agent's voice on the other end of the phone chimed in. Tears streamed down my face. Little did she know the journey I had walking this book out in faith! Long story short, the company had been shifting and changing, and a bunch of manuscripts were overlooked or thrown into the throw-out pile for first-time, unknown authors at the time I had submitted it. After the transition, they had the idea to go back through and look over the ones a previous employee had rejected, and they stumbled upon mine. Am I ever so grateful!

As another testimony of God's goodness over that book, as a first-time author I was asked to invest finances into the project. Guess how much I needed? The exact amount I had raised through my walk-a-thon. God's amazing!

Your Story

What a journey it is to walk things out with the Lord! Whatever you are walking through today, beloved, know that God is right there with you through it. There are some things that we have to pray to break off, and then there are others that we have to walk out or walk through with God, but either way *He is there!*

What pulls us through is being able to grab on to Heaven's perspective. Don't listen to what the natural shows you. That's easy. That doesn't take any faith or maturity. This company of warriors that I saw and believe you are a part of has passed through seasons of testing. The truth is, often what we have victory in has come at a cost, hasn't it?

What we have victory in has come at a cost.

You have walked through moments when you could have given up. You could have melted away in defeat. But you will *not!* I sense right now that many of you are walking through a real faith test. Everything in the natural is screaming at you to pull back, to give up, to quit, to maybe take an easier road.

But God! What does He say? What has He showed you to do? Often, if He hasn't said anything different, then it's a matter of simply walking out what He has shown you.

I remember once walking through something and I had to just keep applying the Word of God to my situation over and over and over again. Declaring, "God, You are going to move this mountain, because this is what Your Word says!" Then I would quote Scripture.

The enemy wants to do everything to get you to agree with him in this season. We have to pull on our heavenly Father: "Daddy, what do You say? What are You going to do? What's Your final answer to this?"

Come on up right now and sit on His lap for a second. You are *"with Him in the heavenly places in Christ Jesus"* (Eph. 2:6), so with boldness you can come and sit up on His lap and ask Him for answers. You are an heir of Christ, so you can sit up on His lap and seek direction and answers. Often, our own perspective on our relationship with the Father is what needs to shift.

He loves you, beloved. You can come boldly before your King Jesus and ask of Him what lies on your heart. The Word says:

> *Ask, and the gift is yours. Seek, and you'll discover. Knock, and the door will be opened for you. For every persistent one will get what he asks for. Every persistent seeker will discover what he longs for. And everyone who knocks persistently will one day find an open door* (Matthew 7:7-8 TPT).

Jesus has an answer. He has a solution. He's creating and moving things whether we can see them or not. God is behind it all.

Some of us are maybe walking through a season right now where we need creative solutions. God gives the most creative blueprints to those of us who can catch His vision. If God can speak through a donkey and also make fish and loaves of bread multiply, clearly He is in the business of creative solutions.

Take a moment and ask the Lord if there is something that He is asking you to do as a prophetic act of investing into your destiny. Now, I realize that walking 33 miles isn't everyone's cup of tea, but He could be asking you to do something else to sow into your promise. God rewards faith acts! Faith acts can move us from a position of being stuck to gaining momentum. Do you want momentum?

> Faith acts can move us from
> a position of being stuck to
> gaining momentum.

Soaring Like an Eagle

The Lord started speaking to me recently about the eagle. I knew that eagles have really stupendous eyesight; they can see and focus in on their prey from miles away. Something unique about eagles that I learned is that as a storm approaches eagles fly directly into the storm, catch the wind from it, and then propel and rise right above it. It's rare to see eagles beat their wings. They catch the wind, stretch out their wings, and soar. They save their energy by catching the wind. What an amazing allegory and demonstration of how we can approach life with the Lord. How many times do I try to do things on my own? Getting flustered by life, I look like a bird who hasn't quite learned the grace of flying yet, beating my wings against the wind. Our goal should not be to avoid storms but simply to rise above them with Him. As we lean into the Lord and gain His perspective, we save our own energy.

> *It is not by force nor by strength, but by my Spirit, says the Lord of Heaven's Armies* (Zechariah 4:6 NLT).

A Prophetic Word: Soaring and Perspective

The Lord spoke this to me very clearly one day: "Everything in the natural screams not now; why now; too much; where's the balance? Come on up here, beloved. Don't look with fear. I'm taking you to the edge of the pinnacle. How will you ever grow without stretching? Come up to the high places where you soar on My wind, not beating your wings; catch My Spirit. Catch My wind. I am behind you, underneath you, and all around you, lifting you up. Not in your own strength can you do this, but in your uninhibited, surrendered trust in Me. We will climb this mountain together, leap from new heights, swim to new depths of understanding My love for you. The one who I love much—why do you fear? Rejoice, soar, laugh, love, rest, find me, surrender, restore. Wings unclipped but fully dependent on my wind. Fearless one, *leap forward!*"

> *Yet those who wait for the Lord will gain new strength; they will mount up with wings like eagles, they will run and not get tired, they will walk and not become weary* (Isaiah 40:31).

As we lean into the Lord and gain His perspective, we save our own energy.

A Prayer for Perspective

> *Lord, give me Your perspective. God, help me to see beyond what I see in front of me. I trust You, God. I may not see it right now, but I know You are leading my life. I can't do this on my own, God. I need You. I choose*

to lean into You and trust You. I'm going to rest in trust. Let my vision not be clouded by my circumstances, my emotions, my health, my fatigue, my finances, my relationships, my setbacks, my surroundings.

I pray now that my vision would be clear to see. I declare Revelation 3:18 over myself; Lord, put eye salve on my eyes so that I can see clearly. I want to rise up higher and see from Your perspective, God. I put my faith in You right now. Give me eyes of faith, God, that see far beyond my current circumstance and that see as You see. Amen.

Jesus Walks in the Middle of Warfare

When we are in real warfare, as I know you might be right now as you're reading this, it's often so hard to be able to shift our perspective off of the warfare. We take hit after hit and think, *God, is this warfare ever going to end?*

Recently, when I was in Maryland speaking at a conference, the Lord showed me that night that there would be significant breakthrough for many people attending the conference. As a seer, I often will see what God wants to do in a meeting beforehand. It's just the way He prepares me for significant moves, so I know how to align myself with where Holy Spirit wants to go and lay down my own agenda or plans.

As I was praying and worshiping in the hotel room alone before I went to head down to the conference, suddenly (out of nowhere) my left hip felt a stabbing sharp pain. I went from a pain scale of zero to a nine in a matter of seconds. Bellowing, I fell to edge of the bed and cried out to God.

"God, take this pain from me. I rebuke you, enemy, from even trying to attack me right now. God, why is this happening? Take it away, God. This is warfare, I just know it. Oh, God, take the pain!" I cried out.

Suddenly, Jesus walked into the room. I was still hunched over the side of the bed when I looked down at the floor and saw the feet of Jesus. I saw His bare feet, holes in his ankles, and the very bottom of what looked like His white linen robes.

"Touch My feet, Ana," I heard His voice say. Nervously, I put my fingers in the holes in His feet and immediately the pain completely left. "This is just warfare, Ana. Keep your eyes on Me," I heard the voice say.

That night at the conference, we saw many healed. New kidneys were released from Heaven, a kid got healed of lymphatic cancer, backs were healed, many were delivered. It was a wonderful night partnering with Jesus! But wow, oh wow, was the warfare strong before!

Every person I have known or studied in history who carried an anointing from the Lord walked through personal battles to get there. Faith is a muscle, and it is stretched and pushed to our limits sometimes, but we gain more authority out of the pressing.

We gain more authority out of the pressing.

You can't have authority in something you haven't walked through personally. It's just not the way it works. The depth of the well of relationship you carry with the Lord is where you can gain any authority.

Shifting Focus

Let's go back to the original vision of the Warrior Bride the Lord showed me at the beginning of this book:

> The oppressive spirits were bigger and stronger than the people, and the people were losing. Then I saw the King of Glory, Jesus Himself, dressed in His royal robes, ride up on a huge white horse. "Rise up! We've gotten off course. Shift your focus. We are winning!"

In the midst of heavy warfare, it's hard to see beyond the war, but we have to look up. We have to find Jesus. As we set our eyes on Him, we realize that we are winning. Even though it may not feel like it now, beloved, *He has crushed satan!* He is our Hope! He is our Victory! He is our strong tower who we can lean on in the middle of the storm.

Let's remember what happened to Peter as he was walking out in faith toward Jesus on top of the sea. As soon as he took his focus off of Jesus and looked at his circumstances, he began to sink.

> *Peter said to Him, "Lord, if it is You, command me to come to You on the water." And He said, "Come!" And Peter got out of the boat, and walked on the water and came toward Jesus. But seeing the wind, he became*

frightened, and beginning to sink, he cried out, "Lord, save me!" (Matthew 14:28-30)

Find *Him* today. Whatever you are walking through, find Him.

Prayer for Perspective

Jesus, I choose to look at You as I walk through the tough valleys or rise to the joyful heights. I set my eyes on You. Let You be what I focus on. Jesus, I just thank You. God, I thank You for the wonderful things You have done in my life. I thank You for what You are doing right now. I thank You for the many blessings I have today. I thank You that I am even breathing right now. I am so grateful, God, for Your loving-kindness. I worship You, God. Up from these ashes I will rise. I will soar with You through my praise. Holy. I set my eyes on You, my King Jesus. You are beautiful in every way. I am so grateful. Amen.

Chapter 6

The Dance of Rest

Many of us have been contending for so long we don't know how to rest. What does rest even look like when you have been battling so long?

By nature, I will admit that I am an overcomer. If there is a challenge presenting itself, I will fight to overcome. It's just the way I'm wired. I've seen fighting at its best and worst—violence in the streets of Brazil, death in the eyes of an infant I held in Mozambique, starvation in the street of Kolkata, India, and the perseverant spirit of a person continuing to push through pain day in and day out. Granted, there are various degrees of fighting we all face, and these are extremes. But each of us have had to face our own personal battles.

The Warrior's Dance

Somewhere along the way, because of surviving through some pretty intense experiences when I had to trust God for my life, I found myself relating to the image of a tough, surviving warrior. It was deep, deep down. I didn't even realize how strong it had been ingrained in me until God began to peel back some of the layers of my heart and take me back to a place of vulnerability. The stripping down process, as I like to call it, was where I learned to rest and trust Him completely.

Can you relate at all? Perhaps you are someone who has survived and faced mountains of discouragementhead-on. Or perhaps you have had to push through many challenges that have come your way because of the cards you were dealt in life. If you can find yourself relating at all, then I encourage you to do as Holy Spirit encouraged me one day: "Lay down your armor," I heard Him say. "Come and learn the dance of rest."

Now there are different seasons and stages the Lord will take us through. There is a season to contend, to declare, to fight against principalities, to take new territory for the Lord; but there are also seasons the Lord will take us to when we sit and lay our head on His chest as John did and rest in Him. It's important to know what season you are in.

Like the eagle soaring, we are not frantically fighting the wind. Some of us have done our part. We have contended, stepped out in faith, prayed the Word of God over our situation, fasted, declared promises of truth, worshiped, repented. You name it, we've done it. And yet here we are, still fighting for our freedom, for our wholeness, to conquer the next mountain.

You were created to shine, beloved. You were created to not just survive life but thrive and enjoy the fullness of life He has for you.

> *But I have come to give you everything in abundance, more than you expect—life in its fullness until you overflow!* (John 10:10 TPT)

An Encounter with Rest[1]

I woke up today feeling sick. My body was sending me a sign, a sign that it was time to rest and step back from a few too many activities and allow my body to restore itself. My throat throughout the day was sore; my voice was scratchy. I just kept going. With two little ones at home, laundry seems endless. *I gotta keep going. I just can't rest,* I thought. I know I'm not alone in this crazy, bizarre type of thinking. I mean, what crazy animals would keep driving themselves into the ground when they are sick or injured? Humans, that's who!

Later, it was ministry night for me at the church. As the associate director of the healing rooms, Tuesday nights are go times for me and my family. I arrive early to help set up, then I walk around the room and prayerfully shift the atmosphere and invite the Presence of God into the room. I make sure every team member has everything they need. I make sure the worship team and sound system are going smoothly. I go over the flow of the night with the other directors of our healing rooms and ask Jesus for direction.

My throat kept hurting. The more I talked, the more it ached. Unconsciously, I kept rubbing my neck where my tonsils are. "Go lie down, Ana," I heard the voice of the Lord command me. So I did just that. In the sanctuary where the live worship was happening, I stretched out on a back row of chairs so as not to be a distraction. I raised my hands to the sky worshiping God. (I must have looked quite odd, but when I'm going after God, hey, who cares what I look like!)

As I stretched my hands up, I suddenly saw a picture. I saw Jesus in an instant. He looked at me, grabbed on to my hands, and blew in my face. This wasn't like a soft, gentle wind. Oh no! It was a mighty wind that sent tingles all the way down my body. It shook me to the core. The breath of God was being poured over me. I noticed then that my throat was no longer hurting. God gave me the strength I needed in that moment to minister and pour out on people who were coming for prayer and also to my team.

I learned two things tonight. Number one: it's okay and necessary to take a step back, lie down, and rightfully so, to take care of myself. God doesn't want slaves, but lovers. Sometimes we can work ourselves too much, forgetting that God values the person over what we can do.

Number two: I've learned in moments of weakness to lean into God. Time and time again I've leaned onto His chest and asked Him, "So God, what do You have to say about this? Please come touch me." Let's not be afraid to lean into God when we need it. He's big enough. He can handle it!

The disciple that Jesus dearly loved was at the right of him at the table and was leaning his head on Jesus (John 13:23 TPT).

More Than Physical Rest

More often than not, most of the battle with resting is mental, isn't it? Resting my body is one thing, but shutting my mind off—that's another! I once heard this metaphor Bob Jones used. It went something like, "Resting isn't just about going across Niagara Falls in a basket; it's about sleeping in that basket while going across Niagara Falls."

I've pondered that metaphor many times. Warfare can be all around you, but maintaining your peace in the midst of it and being unwavering—now that's the real challenge.

While going through a storm, here are some areas where you need to rest:

Rest from Control

When everything seems out of my control, my trust in God really is put to the test. "How much will you trust Me even when you can't see past the storm?" I heard God say to me one day. He is still good. He is still faithful, even though I may not understand. I know someone can relate to this. You've done your part. You may have done everything you know to do, and now it's time to just rest. The situation is out of your control now. You have done your part. Now watch God do His.

Being able to rest really does come down to trusting in Him. I relinquish my control and understanding of the situation and choose to trust in God.

> *God, I surrender my desire to be in control of the situation right now. I may not understand everything, but I know that You love me. You are a good Father*

despite what might happen, and I trust You with my everything. I want You to be in the driver's seat of my life. I know You are in control, and I am choosing to rest today in trust. Amen.

Resting My Mind

Don't be pulled in different directions or worried about a thing. Be saturated in prayer throughout each day, offering your faith-filled requests before God with overflowing gratitude. Tell him every detail of your life, then God's wonderful peace that transcends human understanding, will make the answers known to you through Jesus Christ (Philippians 4:6-7 TPT).

Sometimes it feels like we have to push for rest for our minds, which seems like an oxymoron! As we press in for rest, Jesus give us peace that surpasses all understanding! When nothing makes sense, we can pray for supernatural peace to crash in. Our mind quiets down from trying to figure it all out or find the answers. We become saturated with His Presence. His Presence removes our stress and weariness.

Being saturated in His Presence is like being underwater and looking up into the smiling eyes of Jesus. I just hear the Father saying to you as you're reading this:

Come rest, beloved. Lay down the franticness going on in your mind. Peace, peace. Come now and find rest for your soul. Don't move from My Presence. Learn to stay here.

> **Being saturated in His Presence is like being underwater and looking up into the smiling eyes of Jesus.**

Rest from Doing

This perhaps is one of the hardest things to pull back and rest from. There are seasons God takes us through when we are birthing many things and doing so much with Him. Right now, many of us are in a prophetic birthing season—we are pushing, pressing forward, creating, and dreaming impossible things with God. In that place of doing, though, we have to find rest. We will do more for the Kingdom of God through the place of rest.

I once had a vision of a group of what looked like warriors charging forward. "For the *Kingdom!*" they yelled. Then, Jesus appeared. I watched as they stopped charging and laid down their heads on His chest and rested. "From here, Ana, you find your strength. From here you charge forward. From the place of resting in Me," I heard Him say.

Resting in Him doesn't mean being lazy! You have clear assignments from the Lord right now—perhaps *many* assignments right now all at once. Resting doesn't mean for you to disconnect from those assignments. Resting in Him means fulfilling the assignments God has given you but from a place of deep intimacy with Him and peace.

I recount the scripture about John resting on Jesus' chest.

> *"Truly, truly, I say to you, that one of you will betray Me." The disciples began looking at one another, at a loss to know of which one He was speaking. There was reclining on Jesus' bosom one of His disciples, whom Jesus loved. So Simon Peter gestured to him, and said to him, "Tell us who it is of whom He is speaking." He, leaning back thus on Jesus' bosom, said to Him, "Lord who is it?" Jesus then answered, "That is the one for whom I shall dip the morsel and give it to him"* (John 13:21-26).

The disciples have an agenda. They are trying to figure out who Jesus is talking about. Who is going to betray Jesus? From the place of leaning on His chest, John gets the answer. There is nothing in this life worth more than pursing intimacy with Jesus, and from that place we charge forward with clear direction and strength.

Would you linger, beloved? Would you stay just a little bit longer and rest with Him today? Don't rush forward with the busyness of the day. Imagine just leaning your head on His chest. Let Him just love on you a little longer. Stay close. Stay intimate. Allow God to breathe into you and watch how different your day will be. Just breathe Him in.

Rest from Being Overwhelmed

One of the most impactful encounters that I have ever had with the Lord came from a place of feeling overwhelmed. I was in a season when I had so much going on. My ministry was taking off; my husband and I were co-directing a healing room as well. I was writing a book. I had two beautiful young children under the age of four to care for; I wasn't sleeping very well. It felt like the perfect storm! In every area of my life, I was feeling overwhelmed and at a tipping point. Like, if one more scenario would be added to the load I was carrying, I felt like I would just explode.

I went to the Lord, crying out and, really, complaining. "God, I just don't think I can handle this anymore. I am so overwhelmed right now. Why have You given me this much in this season? Don't You know it's too much for me?"

Right then, in a vision I saw the Lord come to me and hug me. "It's only as overwhelming as you make it," He whispered back in my ear.

It was such a quick impression, but one of the ones that has been the most impactful for my life. Many times, the Lord has brought me back to that encounter as a reminder. Reflecting back on that moment, I had been inwardly making vows with being overwhelmed by saying it: "I'm so overwhelmed right now." As soon as I had that encounter, I immediately repented for even saying that and turned to thank Jesus for all the beautiful blessings He was doing in and through my life in that season.

You know what happened? That feeling of being overwhelmed lifted! Did you catch that? By repenting from even agreeing with being overwhelmed and changing my attitude to one of gratitude, that feeling of being overwhelmed completely broke off of me!

I just declare over you, warrior, that you do not need to be overwhelmed right now. *Yes!* You have a lot going on. You have a lot on your plate of responsibilities, but you do not need to be overwhelmed. He is our strength. He will pull you through this season with *joy!* He has given you what you need to overcome feeling overwhelmed. You *can do this—with Him!*

> *I find that the strength of Christ's explosive power infuses me to conquer every difficulty* (Philippians 4:13 TPT).

Resting in His Love and Him Alone

> *You're my place of quiet retreat, and your wrap-around presence becomes my shield as I wrap myself in your word!* (Psalm 119:114 TPT)

> *Lord, you are a paradise of protection to me. You lift me high above the fray. None of my foes can touch me when I'm held firmly in your wrap-around presence!* (Psalm 61:3 TPT)

I'm a seer, so I'm a pretty visual-concept kind of learner. The description of the Lord's Presence being a "wrap-around" kind of presence always sticks with me. Just imagine the Lord wrapping His Presence around you right now like a warm blanket being thrown around your shoulders.

That's His love. It surrounds you. It protects you. It tucks you into safety. As you pursue knowing His love deeper each day—because there is always more to learn and receive—and resting in it, you will be grounded to withstand any storm.

I have seen trauma literally melt away from people as the love of God crashes over them when we are praying for them. His love melts all our fears, traumas, mistakes, and pain away as we embrace it.

Whose voice are you allowing to speak into you today? It's so important as well that we stay close and only hear the voice of our heavenly Father. God will speak through many people in our lives. The enemy will also try to speak through many people in our lives. So, whose voice are you listening to? Shield yourself in His love, His voice alone, and His Presence.

We can do nothing separate from God. Once again, I remind you today what the Lord reminded me: "Lay down your armor," I heard Him say. "Come and learn the dance of rest."

Stay close to Him. Lean into Him to be your strength today. Find supernatural peace in Him. Gain wisdom and perspective as you rest in Him. Don't rush your time today with Jesus. Just be still and receive from the King. He is doing so much through you right now. Come get nourished and refreshed. Don't be a malnourished, exhausted warrior. Come get strengthened by just being in His Presence. Rest in Him.

Note

1. Ana Werner, *Seeing Behind the Veil* (Shippensburg, PA: Destiny Image Publishers, 2018), 51-52.

Chapter 7

The Dance of Faith

In the vision I had of the warrior Bride, I heard the Lord say, "Find the pulse of Holy Spirit and stay with it. Rise up. Grow louder in your declarations and prayers. Don't you know the power of prayer?"

I pray this section of the book inspires you to keep going forward, to keep pursuing and dreaming with God. I pray courage and faith are imparted to you right now to do the impossible. I pray you would have a renewed boldness to push through every obstacle that might be standing in your way in this very moment and hold on to the promise of the Lord. Beloved, you are that close to breaking through to a promise of God that is over your life and knit into the very destiny Christ has for you!

So then, we must cling in faith to all we know to be true. For we have a magnificent King-Priest, Jesus Christ, the Son of God, who rose into the heavenly realm for us, and now sympathizes with us in our frailty (Hebrews 4:14 TPT).

Moments of Immense Courage

Therefore let us draw near with **confidence** *to the throne of grace* (Hebrews 4:16).

Moments of courage are gems sewn throughout the whole Bible. These characters whom we can look at and think, "Wow, look at what God did through their lives"—each has a similar moment with God. The choice was always there to give up, to step back and quit, to shrink back in fear. But each rose to the occasion, and the reward was great.

Moses Faces Fear

Most of us recall the story of Moses parting the Red Sea and the Israelites walking through it as a big *"wow God"* moment, but I want to bring you back to a smaller story, which often gets overlooked, where Moses faced his fear head-on.

God commissioned Moses to deliver the Israelites from the hands of Pharaoh and the Egyptians, which was a very powerful moment. But Moses had an inner struggle that we see right from the beginning: *"Who am I, that I should go to Pharaoh, and that I should bring the sons of Israel out of Egypt?"* (Exod. 3:11).

"Who am I, that I could do this, God?" he seems to say. Boy, have I faced that inner question before! Except I usually deal with doubt of how something is even possible: "I can't do that, God!"

I love the portion of Scripture where God helped him face fear head-on. God asked him to throw down his staff. The staff transformed into a snake and Exodus 4:3 says Moses *fled* (as I would too, I might add! Snakes are disgusting!). Then the Lord instructed Moses to stretch out his hand and grab it by the tail.

So here's the moment. Don't miss this. Imagine you are Moses in that moment. Now, you may not currently live in an area where snakes are a big deal or threat to your life. I've lived in Africa where they have black mambas (the deadliest snake in the world), and I remember how the Africans reacted to hearing there was a mamba near their meeting! The threat was real! But Moses stretched out his hand and grabbed a creature that was known to be a serious threat to his health; he faced his fear straight on. It was an act of courage. In that moment Moses chose inwardly, "I choose faith in *God* and not *fear* right now. I will trust in You." And then a "suddenly" of God occurred. The supernatural superseded what Moses could see in the natural, and suddenly God broke in!

You may not be looking a viper square in the eyes right now, but you have a choice. Will you trust in God? Will you trust that He is good even when you can't understand? Will you trust in God even when the path is unclear or the "how" hasn't been answered yet? Will you trust in God when there is a lot at stake—when there is a high level of risk? Perhaps what God is calling you to do could very well cost you everything. Would you still do it?

Esther's Risk

Let's take a look at Esther's story. The story of Esther has got to be one of my all-time favorites in the Bible—it's the story of someone who is destined for greatness. Did you catch that phrase? I think every newborn baby should get a onesie with that phrase written on it—*destined for greatness!*

Esther had her date with destiny. Through an unusual circumstance, Esther became queen. A powerful man named Haman put out a horrible plot to completely annihilate the Jewish people. Mordecai, Esther's uncle, encouraged her to use her powerful position to approach the king and beg him to save the Jewish people.

He spoke to her this famous line: "*And who knows whether you have not attained royalty for such a time as this?*" (Esther 4:14). You can read the rest of the story, and I truly do encourage you to reread it even if you have read it several times. Mordecai nudged Esther toward her destiny when she felt like she was facing an impossibility.

Then she prepared and approached the king in an act of immense courage. "*Thus I will go in to the king, which is not according to the law; and if I perish, I perish*" (Esther 4:16). As she approached him, it says, "*When the king saw Esther the queen standing in the court, she obtained favor in his sight; and the king extended to Esther the golden scepter*" (Esther 5:2).

Perhaps this is your nudge toward your destiny. You are facing something that requires immense faith. It may require a miracle or a move of God. This is your moment to step up into the ring and chose faith. You have nothing to lose but everything to gain in Christ Jesus. He is for you, not against you. I imagine Him much like King Ahasuerus extending his golden scepter toward Esther, which gave her access to the throne. King Jesus is extending to you this invitation to approach Him with confidence and boldness and ask for what you need. Some of us have been contending for so long, it takes immense courage to muster up enough faith to even ask God again for our breakthrough. Don't you quit! Keep going forward toward the throne of grace and petitioning the King!

> ## Don't you quit! Keep going forward toward the throne of grace and petitioning the king!

Set yourself on worshiping Him with your whole life, and you will find favor follows you.

Joshua's Supernatural Plan from God

Let's look at Joshua's story. God gave Joshua an incredible supernatural plan of victory in a grim situation. After Moses went on to glory with the Lord and passed away, Joshua had the task to lead the Israelites into the promised land.

God encouraged Joshua, *"Be strong and courageous, for you shall give this people possession of the land which I swore to their fathers to give them. Only be strong and very courageous"* (Josh. 1:6-7). *Be strong and courageous* is a word many of us need to be reminded right now.

The Lord instructed Joshua and the Israelites how to conquer what seems like an indestructible city:

> *You shall march around the city, all the men of war circling the city once. You shall do so for six days. ... Then on the seventh day you shall march around the city seven times, and the priests shall blow the trumpets. It shall be that when they make a long blast with the ram's horn, and when you hear the sound of the trumpet, all the people shall shout with a great shout; and the wall of the city will fall down flat, and the people will go up every man straight ahead* (Joshua 6:3-5).

God gave Joshua what seemed in the natural to be a weird idea. Joshua's response may have been, "So You're telling me, God, that I'm going to tell my men here to march around the walls of Jericho for seven days and on that last day to do it seven times, and then we are going to blow our horns and shout and all the walls will fall down....and this is Your strategy for battle, Lord?"

Strategies of the Lord often don't make sense in the natural. God reveals to us creative strategies to every problem or every circumstance we may be facing. Even now, God always has the answer, whether we understand it or not. His instructions don't always make sense or may even seem like they are not going to make a difference, but that is where our faith needs to kick in. It takes faith to believe in God's ways and not in our own strength. When you have done everything you know of to change your circumstance, then God takes your obedience and says, "*Watch who I am, and what I'm about to do.*"

I sense that the Lord is releasing creative strategies to you right now. Pray this prayer to receive them:

> *Lord, I pray for Your creative strategies to be released right now. God, You have the answer to how this great promise You have given me will come to be. Whatever is blocking me from reaching my destiny, I pray for it to be removed right now in Jesus' name. I may not need to know all the steps, but Lord, would You show me the next step in my path? Thank You, Lord. Amen.*

Ruth's Vulnerability

Let's take a look at Ruth's story. Ruth had lost everything. Her husband had passed; she lost her home, her stability, her income, and her inheritance. Through her mother-in-law Naomi's instruction, she risked everything on a kinsman of her late husband—Boaz. She gleaned from his fields, and, encouraged by Naomi, she did something that took immense courage.

> *When Boaz had eaten and drunk and his heart was merry, he went to lie down at the end of the heap of grain; and she came secretly, and uncovered his feet and lay down. It happened in the middle of the night that the man was startled and bent forward; and behold, a woman was lying at his feet. He said, "Who are you?" And she answered, "I am Ruth your maid. So spread your covering over your maid, for you are a close relative"* (Ruth 3:7-9).

According to custom, Boaz could marry Ruth and basically save her from the destiny of being a poor widow. She had no sons, so in that time and age—no inheritance. Without his help and marriage, she had no real future. So, following the wisdom of her mother-in-law, in the middle of the night she did something that took an immense amount of courage and also vulnerability. Boaz woke up in the middle of the night and found a woman lying down beside him. Can you imagine the possible outcomes for this scenario? Boaz could have not only rejected her but also shamed her to the community, but it worked out in Ruth and Naomi's favor. Boaz took her in as his wife.

Perhaps your walk of faith in this hour is one that would require immense vulnerability and risk from you.

The Disciples' Immediate Obedience

Lastly, when Jesus first approached Simon Peter and Andrew fishing on the shoreline, He called them out:

> *"Follow Me, and I will make you fishers of men."*
> ***Immediately*** *they left their nets and followed Him*
> (Matthew 4:19-20).

The disciples had everything to lose. Fishing was their income—their livelihood. Who was this guy, anyway, telling them to put down their nets and follow Him? Obviously, we know this man was Jesus, Son of God, but did they in that very moment? Their pure, hundred-percent obedience in that very moment to lay down everything they knew is what always astonishes me.

If God was calling you to do something today that would take incredible faith like that, would you obey? Would you have faith that says, "I'm willing to risk it all for You, God; I may not understand where You are taking me, but I trust that You are good and you are leading"? Could we completely lay down our own agendas and plans for God's right now?

The Sound of Faith

"We became victorious as we matched His sound." This part of the vision that God gave me I have meditated and thought over many times. In the vision, our ability to become victorious was directly correlated with matching the sound of the Father.

So what is God saying about your current situation? Many of us may be looking straight up the mountainside of an impossible dream. We may not even be on the journey climbing up that mountain, but just at the bottom looking up at that steep slope. Perhaps you have just walked through a tough season of what feels like many setbacks. The finances aren't there or the family relationships aren't peaceful; the helpers and support to make this dream come true are missing. Your work is not where you wished it would be. Perhaps your marriage is going through a rough time. Perhaps you are pioneering through what feels like an uphill trench. Or maybe your health is not where you wished it would be. All of these examples can feel like a giant mountain standing in front of you, like an obstacle blocking you from reaching your goals.

> *Listen to the truth I speak to you: If someone says to this mountain with great faith and having no doubt, "Mountain, be lifted up and thrown into the*

midst of the sea," and believes that what he says will happen, it will be done. This is the reason I urge you to boldly believe for whatever you ask for in prayer— believe that you have received it and it will be yours (Mark 11:23-24 TPT).

With a word, God spoke Heaven and earth into existence. Now, I'm not God, but you and I are created in His image. Our words have more power behind them than we realize. So our ability to match the sound of Heaven—or match what God says about our current situation and make declarations into it—shifts what we cannot see with our natural eyes. Speaking over our warfare or struggle with what the enemy already says about it doesn't take any faith. That's easy, actually. But God is raising up an army of people who make declarations in faith that will shift mountains.

So, what does God say about your current situation? "I am a God of the impossible! Believe!"

Beloved, don't give in or listen to the voice of the enemy today. He is a liar and deceiver and he wants you to be paralyzed in fear instead of faith. *Rise up!* Speak to your mountain. Make a declaration in faith over it.

Praying over the Land

"Go there and put your feet in the soil. Pray over it," I heard the Lord say to me one day. It was similar to when Joshua sent out two spies to *"Go, view the land"* (Josh. 2:1). Many times, the Lord has summoned me to go to a specific location, put my feet in the soil there, and pray over the land. There is power in our prayers. There is something to praying into and over a specific location the Lord is assigning you to minister in— whether it be a new job, new country, or just a place you want to see God move in that has felt dry of His Presence.

> *Therefore I say to you, all things for which you pray and ask, believe that you have received them, and they will be granted you* (Mark 11:24).

Prayers and acts of faith sometimes require us letting go of our pride and our own understanding. Are you praying for your son or daughter's future spouse right now? Perhaps God will call you to do something that in the natural seems so silly—like go to a bridal shop and pray for the right spouse God has for them.

Let me back up and give you more details about the purchase of our house. As we were looking at houses, one house in the natural looked like a dump. It was a really outdated home that needed not just "a lot of love" but more like a total overhaul. The previous owner also had been a bit of a hoarder, so walking through it was nearly impossible. And yet this home stood out to me and I felt peace there that I hadn't with the previous ones we had walked through.

"I need some time alone to walk through it," I told my husband. The real estate agent waited outside for a few minutes, and my husband corralled the kiddos outside so I could walk through it alone.

I prayed, "Jesus if this is the house You have for us, I declare over it a house of peace. A place of settling for us as a family. I declare that this will be a place of ministry and also a place of respite. I declare that every financial hurdle we may have to go through to be able to purchase this house is removed. I declare that every obstacle be removed for us to get this house. I pray for favor with the banks. Lord, give us a vision to see beyond the junk that I see before me now. I declare that this house will sparkle!"

We put in an offer for the house that day, and after many hurdles, which you read about earlier, we got the house. Today that house "sparkles" indeed! It took a lot of faith, a lot of hard work, and a lot of love to make it sparkle, but looking back I have to think, "*Wow God!* Look what You did!" When we put an offer on the house, it seemed like an impossible dream. But God moved mountains, and we got it.

Today, maybe the Lord is asking you to physically go somewhere, put your feet on the soil, and pray over it a prayer filled with faith. As faith is the currency of Heaven, think of it as like you are sowing into the ground and watering it with Heaven's blessings.

Working that Faith Muscle: Sowing, Sacrifice, and Reaping

For what you plant will always be the very thing you harvest (Galatians 6:7 TPT).

The notion of sowing and planting and then reaping has been around since farmers planted the first seed. As we step out and work our muscles of faith, we also need to be sowing into the place we want to reap in.

Back when the Lord called me to the mission field of Brazil, I remember hearing His voice, "Sow into the country,

Ana." I began to pray about how to sow into Brazil before I physically went. I purchased a program to learn the language, so I sowed financially and also with my time to learn the language. Then I prayed and asked the Lord to show me ministries in Brazil working with street children that I could sow my finances into to bless. Lastly, I started daily praying over the country and its people.

With every drop you are sowing, you will reap later. It might be years later, but you will reap the benefits eventually. People who have immense blessing of the Lord over their lives have sown and blessed others significantly. When we look at the way farmers plow the land, water the land, plant the seeds, pick the weeds, and then finally collect the harvest, one thing sure does come to mind—*sweat!* Harvesting takes a lot of hard work and sacrifice. Sacrifice never is easy and always requires faith.

How can you plant a seed offering today? Look at the promise God has for you that you are contending for right now, as if surveying the land. How can you sow into that promise today?

> *May he remember every gift you have given him and celebrate every sacrifice of love you have shown him* (Psalm 20:3 TPT).

Dreaming Again

Okay, all this sounds great—acts of faith, sowing in faith, praying in faith. But what if you've been waiting so long now that just thinking of that promise makes you sick to the stomach with the delay?

For some of us, it's a real step of faith to even begin to dream again with God. After many setbacks, or perhaps unfulfilled promises, optimistically believing that God can do a miracle right now can seem pretty far-fetched.

One day, I was taken into a vision of a room in Heaven with God. (I like to call this the creation room.) There I saw before me what looked like a giant screen. Jesus was there drawing on it, and colors moved and swirled creatively. "Come," He said. "Let's begin to dream again." With that, the two of us put our hands to the screen, and I watched as dreams I had kept hidden deep, deep down in my heart began to surface and appear on the screen. He looked at me, and I heard a voice say, "I haven't forgotten."

"I haven't forgotten."

That's when I realized it. Dreams I had from way back when, I had placed on a shelf somewhere and forgotten about them. Years of waiting had moved me toward disbelief that these things were even possible anymore, and I had just laid them down as impossibilities.

Even now as I am writing this, I sense that many people who may read this are in a season right now when you need to pick up old dreams. It's not that the dreams have been forgotten or that God has closed a door; it's just that it may have morphed and changed direction a bit. The ministry or calling is not forgotten; it has just transformed.

It takes faith and courage to dream again. Have courage. To believe and ask the question, "But what if, God—what if?" I remember hearing Patricia King say, "What you can see, you can have," and I remember thinking at first, *Well, that's very optimistic.* But you know what the Lord showed me? She's right! See, I needed to stretch my faith and dream much bigger and larger with God, and this very statement stretched me to the next level in faith. God was pushing me to grow.

What are you dreaming with God today? Is it something that could be possible in your own strength? I want to encourage you to dream much bigger than your own strength. Begin to dream the dreams that are impossible without God's intervention.

Prayer of Faith

> *Lord, endue us with faith to pick up old dreams off the shelf and believe again that anything is possible with You! Give us courage now to dream much bigger and larger than anything we could do ourselves. God, show us Your vision for the impossible. Show us what it is You want to do through our little lives to bring forth Your Kingdom.*

The image of a warrior and the image of a dreamer don't seem to go together, right? But I believe a seasoned warrior has a level of faith to move mountains, to press through any obstacle and any fear, and strength to keep their eyes on what the Lord has called them to create and do. They won't stop at any setback; they continue to press into the Lord for strength.

The warrior's very cry is, "*But my God!*" as they declare into their situation and watch Heaven's response.

Do you have faith for the impossible, beloved? It's time to begin to dream.

Stepping Forward and Possessing the Land

So how, then, do we move forward and take the land or promise of God?

Many of us have heard a word of the Lord. In faith we have stood and declared, "It shall be in Jesus' name." We've spoken the Word of God over our situation, releasing declarations that are shifting things in the supernatural. God has shown us a clear vision and direction. He's given us blueprints for the future. He's even opening doors that only God could open in our lives.

It's time now to walk through and take possession of the promised land. Right as we are on the brink of stepping over into that promised land, there is always the possibility of being swallowed by fear.

As the Israelites crossed through the Red Sea, it wasn't enough for them to have faith to walk through a body of water that was "*like a wall to them on their right hand and on their left*" (Exod. 14:22). That in itself would have filled me with terror! But as they trekked through it (which wasn't like a two-minute walk either!) they did so with the Egyptians racing behind them through the ocean walls in pursuit! *Fear* is always in pursuit of us when we are on the brink of breakthrough. Did you catch that?

> *Fear* is always in pursuit of us when we are on the brink of breakthrough!

So have you felt recently like you are swallowed or over-whelmed with fear? The enemy wants to paralyze you in fear, to keep you from possessing that promise of God over your life. I want to encourage you to do as the Israelites did. As you walk toward that promise of God—*just keep going forward.* Don't quit. Don't let fear be what keeps you from greatness. And keep your focus on Jesus and the goal line. Gain some tenacity today to press through the narrow place.

After Moses and the Israelites crossed through the Red Sea, it's important to see that God asked Moses to stretch his hand out over that sea so that the waters would fall over the Egyptians and wipe them out (see Exod. 14:26). Similarly, God instructed the Israelites when they crossed over the Jordan to drive out all the inhabitants of the land and destroy all of their false idols (see Num. 33:51-52).

When we battle in the spirit to take on new land or new ter-ritory with the Lord, it's so important that we clean house. It starts with me first—keeping my own heart pure and clean of sin. When we "cross over" or walk through the doors of oppo-sition and into that promise of God for which we have been contending for so long, let's sanctify that promise as unto the Lord. Let's dedicate it as His.

I remember when my husband and I were missionaries in India. We lived in a place of strong spiritual warfare, where Hindu temples surrounded our flat. Idol worship was rampant all around us. I remember when we moved in, I felt a nudge from Holy Spirit to pray a cleansing prayer over our flat, to declare it as a place of peace and the Lord's house, and declare that the blood of the Lamb had washed it clean.

I encourage you now to do the same over your promise of God.

> *Lord, first we are so grateful that You are calling us now to walk in and take possession of our promised land. I dedicate this promise as Yours, God, and ask You to have Your way with it. Lord, keep my heart clean and pure and worshipful as I walk through this door toward my destiny. God, I plead the blood of the Lamb over myself, my family, and all that I have, and I ask You to wash us clean. Make me a pure and holy vessel. And I thank You, Lord. Amen.*

Chapter 8

The Dance of Humility, Honor, and Accountability

Although not always a popular topic, honor, humility, servanthood, and submission to accountability are all part of the warrior's DNA. In my vision:

> I was hearing the sound from the Father and repeating it back on my little instrument. It was slow and steady at first, and then as the army of Christ joined with me it grew *loud* and faster! Our sound broke louder than the clash of the enemy's assaults. And we grew strong!

There we were, sounding our little drums together, making a loud sound that broke the sounds and assaults of the enemy. It wasn't one sound that could break the assaults, but together we could fight.

Accountability and working as a team are irreplaceable as the war increases. We are in this together. The enemy tries his best to make us feel isolated in our battles.

The Coming Together

The motto of the US Marines is "*Semper Fidelis,*" which means *always faithful.* Their faithfulness to serve the team is quite honorable. We are all called to shine but also called to serve one another.

Jesus displayed an act of love with the disciples by washing their feet, knowing that this would be one of the last things He would leave them with. Imagine, there He was, about to face the cross, knowing the suffering He was about to go through. And Jesus thought, "I know what I want to teach them. I want to show them the importance of servanthood." At least, that's how it plays out in my head.

> *Jesus, knowing that the Father had given all things into His hands, and that He had come forth from God and was going back to God, got up from supper, and laid aside His garments; and taking a towel, He girded Himself. Then He poured water into the basin, and began to wash the disciples' feet and to wipe them with the towel with which he was girded. ..."If I then, the*

Lord and the Teacher, washed your feet, you also ought to wash one another's feet" (John 13:3-5,14).

The Lord wants to release His Presence in full measure over every area of the world, into every area of society. From the small child who sits on the streets begging for food, to the single mom working two jobs to support her family, to the businessman who sits at the top of his game on Wall Street, to the overworked father working for the power company—God wants to break out! God wants every person in every nation to come to know Him (see Phil. 2:11).

It will take all the different streams coming together to win all souls for Jesus. As we come together in humility, love, and honor as Jesus did, we can have greater impact. Perhaps you are not in ministry and may be thinking, *What is she talking about?* Individualism is on the rise in society right now, but we have to live our lives according to the Word of God and not go along with the societal norm. I am not talking here about rebelling against society. No! I want to match my heart's posture as close as I can to that of Jesus, and He valued all the differences of the disciples and loved them!

When I lived overseas as a missionary, the most disheartening thing to see was when ministries would strive against each other almost in competition. I would sit back and wonder, "Hey, we all love Jesus and want to reach the lost. Why does our ministry seem like your enemy? Can't we work together somehow?" From an outside perspective, it always seemed like the ministries in those areas could have accomplished so much more if they found a way to work together to reach the lost. We can't do it alone. God wants to reach *every* person in the entire universe with His love. I don't know about you, but I know I can't reach every nation alone.

When It Works

And He gave some as apostles, and some as prophets, and some as evangelists, and some as pastors and teachers. for the equipping of the saints for the work of service, to the building up of the body of Christ; until we all attain to the unity of the faith, and of the knowledge of the Son of God, to a mature man, to the measure of the stature which belongs to the fullness of Christ...from whom the whole body, being fitted and held together by what every joint supplies, according to the proper working of each individual part, causes the growth of the body for the building up of itself in love (Ephesians 4:11-13,16).

One night during a tour with Sid Roth in Israel in 2019, something beautiful occurred. An unplanned meeting of worship and prophecy broke out. I was up on stage ministering and witnessed as Holy Spirit took over the meeting. What was beautiful to watch was how each of us leaders would minister in our own unique ways and there was a convergence of the fivefold ministry. We had a prophetic teacher, a pastor, an apostle, a prophetic seer, and a worship leader all up there on stage following the leading of the Holy Spirit. All we needed was Sid to be up there with us that night and we would have had the evangelist too!

What was beautiful to witness was how each of us would follow the leading of the Lord in an orchestrated flow that worked together. At one point I (the seer) got a vision of what God was about to do. I looked at the apostle and said, "You're carrying a word from the Lord right now, and an explosion of the Lord's Presence is about to break out through that word." As my friend the apostle then nodded in agreement and stood forward to release a word of the Lord, the rest of us stood back out of honor and also to receive what he had to say. One by one, as Holy Spirit would instruct, we each had our part to play in what happened that night. One would release a teaching, the other a prophetic word, I would release vision for what God was doing around the room, the other a prophetic song that would bring the anointing down.

There was no strife to rise above the other. No dishonor. No disharmony. All were unified by the purpose of bringing the Kingdom of God to earth. Each of us knew our place, knew who we were in Christ, knew the authority we carried, embraced the uniqueness that each of us brought, and honored each other, and *wow, did God break out!* This was a taste of the army I saw the Lord raising up.

A Taste of Heaven

God does raise up individuals who will pioneer and be forerunners—yes! But no one warrior is to stand alone isolated and be ambushed by the enemy's assaults. God wants to release His Presence in an unprecedented measure, and our timeline is speeding up to the day of His return. We can do more in a shorter amount of time if we are doing it together.

Generations Running Together

Not only are all the different streams of ministry and the fivefold important, but the different generations are also valuable. In my vision of the great army, I saw many different age groups running forward together in the battle and winning! This is a key to the greatest outpouring of the Spirit of God on the earth. The different generations have to come together.

Mentors, Accountability, and Vulnerability

You might ask, "What would that look like?" Vulnerability and mentorship are irreplaceable. I personally have a mentor who speaks into my life. I willingly allow this person to get close enough to me to challenge me, push me, hold me accountable, and get really raw and vulnerable with me. The ability to be vulnerable with someone else and share the inner things that I am praying and working through has been one of the most valuable relationships I have. Not only do they pray for me and challenge me, my mentors have called me out at times when I needed it and said, "Ana, this is who you are! Don't let the enemy say otherwise!" Mentoring, I believe, is calling someone up to a higher place.

> **Mentoring is calling someone up to a higher place.**

As social media has boomed, the pressure for performance or looking good has also risen. *Pride* has always been an issue since satan fell from Heaven; it just might look different depending on the era.

> *For the Lord of hosts will have a day of reckoning against everyone who is proud and lofty and against everyone who is lifted up, that he may be abased* (Isaiah 2:12).

It takes great courage and vulnerability to be willing to be mentored, but we have everything to gain from it. Choose wisely whom you allow into your life to mentor you. It's wisdom to align yourself with a person who has years of experience, but also someone you see bearing really good fruit.

Perhaps right now you don't have a mentor yet and are realizing you need one. I'm going to pray for you, reader, if you find yourself in this position.

> *Lord, I pray right now in this season You would raise up the right leader or mentor for my friend here. Raise up someone (or someones) who will nudge them always toward greater purpose, greater measures of faith, and who will help bring out the best in them. You always have a divine plan, Lord, so I pray You would bring forth the one You have personally chosen to mentor them in this season. Amen.*

I once walked through a very hard experience of being deserted by a really good mentor, and it left me feeling abandoned. Later, when I felt led to reach out to someone else to mentor me, old feelings of fear crept up. *What if this doesn't work out?* I found myself thinking. God had to speak to me in that moment: "Ana, today is a new day! It's okay to be vulnerable again. This will help you!"

If you are recalling past times when perhaps a mentor deserted you or that relationship didn't work out the way you expected, I speak the same thing to you—*today is a new day!*

Honor Between the Generations

When I saw this army God is raising up and I saw the different generations running together, that's when I realized how important honor is. Not only were the younger generations honoring the older generations and valuing their wisdom, the older generations were honoring and valuing what the younger generations brought to the table. These warriors were concerned with the long-term vision of serving the Body of Christ.

Ruth and Naomi are the perfect example from the Bible of what generations running together could look like. Ruth honored her mother-in-law, Naomi, by staying with her when she was urged to leave: *"For where you go, I will go, and where you lodge, I will lodge"* (Ruth 1:16).

Ruth gleaned wisdom from her mother-in-law as she was instructed how to interact with Boaz (see Ruth 3:1-5). Boaz then not only redeemed Ruth by taking her as his wife, he also supplied for Naomi as well. Security was provided for both Ruth and Naomi. They needed each other!

We have much to learn from each other. We need each other to get the job done!

I believe this is what Heaven will look like. All the generations, races, and sexes will all be united, looking and gazing up into the eyes of the one we love—our King Jesus! We will be united in our adoration.

> *The reward of humility and the fear of the Lord are riches, honor and life* (Proverbs 22:4).

Chapter 9

The Dance of Joy

Let's look at two of my favorite scriptures in the whole Bible and an encounter I had with Jesus concerning them.

> *You will make known to me the path of life; in Your presence is fullness of joy; in Your right hand there are pleasures forever* (Psalm 16:11).

> *You prepare a table before me in the presence of my enemies; You have anointed my head with oil; my cup overflows. Surely goodness and lovingkindness will follow me all the days of my life, and I will dwell in the house of the Lord forever* (Psalm 23:5-6).

The idea of a joyful warrior might seem like a bit of an oxymoron, but I assure you it is not. Keeping your joy is actually one of the strongest weapons a warrior has.

Seated at the Banquet Table

That week was a very rough week for me as a mother. I had a newborn baby, so I was already pretty exhausted from lack of sleep. Not only that, my new son had many stomach problems we couldn't figure out for the first couple of months, which led to so much guilt as a mother because I couldn't figure him out. The enemy was truly wearing me down. I prayed over my son, laid hands on him and declared his healing, prayed Scripture over him, worshiped. I also did everything in the natural to help the situation—change my diet drastically, etc. Nothing was working, and I was exhausted.

"God, I don't know what else to do. I've done everything I know," I cried out to God.

"Oh, taste and see that I am good," I heard the Lord's voice say to me one day. Suddenly, I found myself seated at a giant wooden table in Heaven. Jesus was seated across from me. *This is my moment*, I thought. *I'm sitting at the table with Jesus before me, and all I can think about is asking Him what to do about my son.* Lovingly, He looked at me, knowing my thoughts. He smiled and just laughed. "Let's just eat together. Taste and see that I am good," He said.

It was then that I noticed before me a beautiful feast of food set on the table—some foods I had seen before, and some were completely different than any earthly food I had ever seen. It wasn't actually until He spoke that I noticed the bountiful display right before my eyes. I had been so focused on my inward problems that I missed the goodness of God accessible to me.

Jesus' eyes captivated me so much that I had to lay down my agenda right then and there and just enjoyed His company. His eyes require the world to stop and adore.

> ## His eyes require the world to stop and adore.

We feasted together and ended up laughing and laughing together. His bubbling laughter and joy was so contagious. He was never laughing at me or mocking me. He was so full of joy and happiness that laughter just spilled out of Him like a full teapot. As I ate with Him, I started to feel better. I even caught myself laughing and giggling with Him over life. My joy was being replenished.

My son was eventually completely healed of all stomach problems, but what was healed first was my own heart in the middle of what felt like a battle.

God Is Still Full of Joy

I left that encounter feeling so full. The problems of the day hadn't gone away; in fact, as the day carried on they intensified. What had changed tremendously was how I responded to them and my ability to keep my joy despite everything. Would you believe what I flipped my Bible open to that day to read? Psalm 16:11!

When we are in the middle of spiritual warfare, the tendency is to push through, persevere, and fight! All of that is great, but with *joy?* How does that fit the tool belt?

There will always be a war until the day of His return.

> *For our struggle is not against flesh and blood, but against the rulers, against the powers, against the world forces of this darkness, against the spiritual forces of wickedness in the heavenly places* (Ephesians 6:12).

Do you know what, though? God's still full of joy! For many of us, especially if we are walking through a hard season right now, this can be hard to understand. His nature is full of joy despite whatever we might be facing, because by the power of the cross He's *already won*. He crushed satan; it's done! For this reason, through Jesus we can have joy.

I should add here that God having joy doesn't mean that He lacks compassion or empathy for your situation. It's very contrary to that actually. Out of compassion, He sent His only Son for us. Through Jesus' resurrection we have hope for the future. He's won the victory.

Do you know God has so much joy over you? He looks at you and bubbles up with love and joy!

Joy in Unusual Places

I want to share three places where supernatural joy hit me in a way that was unexplainable, changed the atmosphere, and brought the Presence of the Lord. I watched joy being used as a weapon against the assaults of the enemy, stripping down any power he had to be there.

The Wailing Wall in Israel

It was my first time at the Wailing Wall in Israel. This location in Israel is thought to be a holy place. Many people travel from very far to place their prayers rolled up in little pieces of paper in the cracks of the walls. Many believe that this is the closest they can get to the Lord's Presence. I witnessed first-hand why it's called the Wailing Wall, as many gather there to lay hands on the wall and cry out in tears for God to hear their prayers. It's quite sobering actually.

I went up to the wall placed my hands on it and prayed a declaration prayer that went something like this: "Lord, let this nation know Your glory. Let these people know the freedom of You. Let your Presence fall here today. God, may these people here come to know You intimately and hear Your voice for themselves. Lord, break through!"

And there in that place, joy hit me. Suddenly, I felt a rush of supernatural joy shoot through me. Embarrassingly, I had to pull back from the wall. Others were crying out to God around me, and yet I was hearing His heart for His people.

"I love them! I love them! I'm coming, I'm coming!" I heard Him say. And I felt the Lord's joy for them in that moment, and I bubbled up with laughter.

It felt like the most uncomfortable place to receive joy, but God wanted to break out. He was shifting the atmosphere.

Paralyzed Man

Another time supernatural joy burst unexpectedly out of me was when my husband and I were praying over a paralyzed man in Africa. We spent a week in South Africa on our way back to the States, after being on the mission field in Mozambique. Visiting a local church, a man came up for prayer in a wheelchair. Respectfully, we waited until after the service to approach the man and ask him if we could pray for him. To this day, it was one of the most unusual healing testimonies I have a firsthand account for.

As we prayed, the Lord asked me to sing over him. So I started to sing a worship song over him, and although I may not have the sweetest of voices, the Lord's Presence came in a huge way. The man started to feel waves of God's Presence hit him, and he started getting more mobility in his arms and neck.

Then a sudden burst of joy hit me, and I started laughing. I quickly apologized and explained how I wasn't laughing at his health, but God was touching me and sometimes I giggle when that happens. He ended up laughing a bit with me. As we all laughed together and then prayed some more. He was healed.

I am convinced that the joy of the Lord assisted in his healing in that case. He walked out of that wheelchair that day! And guess what? It was his birthday too!

Revival Joy

I was at a revival meeting recently. In the middle of my preaching about freedom with Holy Spirit, joy started breaking out all over the room. If you have never been in a meeting like this where joy breaks out, let me tell you—the first time you experience it, it can be a little offensive and uncomfortable.

There I was preaching, and a few people from the crowd randomly started laughing. Their laughter was contagious, and more people caught it and started laughing. Holy Spirit was up to something fun! It's like He was saying, "You're preaching about freedom with Me! Now I'm going to demonstrate it!" That church had previously been through a really hard week. Joy broke out in that meeting, and as people embraced in it and even stood up and started dancing in joy, healing and miracles broke out all over the meeting.

I do believe the saying, "Laughter is good medicine to our soul," as I've witnessed firsthand how supernatural joy can shift an atmosphere and bring healing.

Choosing Joy

You might be thinking, *Okay. Okay. But choosing joy right now isn't that easy.* I know; I've been there myself. Let me share with you a story from my previous book, *Seeing Behind the Veil*, that might help you with choosing joy. It helped me heaps.

It was a rough season my husband and I were going through in our marriage. We were in Mozambique, Africa as missionaries. Missions has an interesting way of bringing out the best of a person—and also the fleshly worst. The daily challenges stretch you in ways you never even imagined being stretched!

The Warrior's Dance

I'll never forget it. We were invited to a special marriage-celebration-prophetic service; and in all honesty (I truly do love my husband dearly), in that moment I didn't even want to go with him. We had the opportunity to experience something amazing for our marriage, but as warfare often comes before breakthrough, that morning we were at odds with each other.

So there I was in our little living quarters before the event, complaining to the Lord. "I don't want to go to this prophetic thing, God. I don't even want to be there. I'm hurt."

Just like that, a twelve-foot angel showed up and stood over me. Its presence knocked me flat on my back, landing me on the bed. It carried a large trumpet in one hand. Looking at me, it smiled, blew that trumpet right in my face, and declared, "The joy of the Lord is your strength!"

I felt that trumpet blast throughout my body when the sound was released over me. Guess what happened? I was so full of the joy of the Lord that my husband had to help me walk to the flatbed (our mode of transportation, similar to a large truck but not as luxurious!) that would take us to the event. As I literally rolled into the flatbed laughing, I lay down and touched the feet of my friends—other married couples going to the event—and the joy of the Lord splashed onto them. When we reached our destination, all of us tumbled out of the vehicle so full of the joy of the Lord—and so in love with our spouses.

Ever since that encounter with the angel, I have learned so much about the powerful weapon of joy! Times when I have seen the enemy come and try to bring division, discouragement, oppression, set people off course, depression, sickness, and offense, the enemy's weapons are defueled by the power of joy!

Joy is one of the most overlooked weapons against the enemy's assaults, but it's got to be one of my personal favorites. As we focus on Jesus in the middle of our circumstances in the middle of the battlefield and *find Him*, we get filled with joy.

Look at the same scripture I used earlier, Psalm 16:11, in *The Passion Translation*:

> *For you bring me a continual revelation of resurrection life, the path to the bliss that brings me face-to-face with you.*

As we come face to face with Jesus and fix our eyes on Him, He renews us. He brings us joy and refreshment in the middle of the battlefield. He gives you strength to face today. It is a choice though! There are those days when I have to remind myself, "Today, I chose *joy!*"

Today, I choose joy!

I might even say it several times throughout the day as my reminder. I make the choice that no matter the battlefield before my eyes in the natural, I'm going to set my focus on Jesus and meditate on Him instead. And He fills me up with joy despite my circumstances, and the weapons of the enemy suddenly melt off of me.

> *Whatever is true, whatever is honorable, whatever is right, whatever is pure, whatever is lovely, whatever is of good repute, if there is any excellence and if anything worthy of praise, dwell on these things* (Philippians 4:8).

As you focus on the King and choose joy, He wraps His loving-kindness around you (see Ps. 64). He speaks value over us and reminds us how He sees us and who we are; He pours His love into us. I look into those eyes, and I am melted by His pure love. Why wouldn't I lay my life down for Him? Whatever circumstance I am going through, I have to lay it aside and find inner peace and joy as I look toward Him.

> *The joy of the Lord is your strength* (Nehemiah 8:10).

> *And the disciples were continually filled with joy and with the Holy Spirit* (Acts 13:52).

> *For the kingdom of God is not eating and drinking, but righteousness and peace and joy in the Holy Spirit* (Romans 14:17).

> *For even during a season of severe difficulty and tremendous suffering, they became even more filled with joy. From the depths of their extreme poverty, super-abundant joy overflowed into an act of extravagant generosity* (2 Corinthians 8:2 TPT).

Prayer for Supernatural Joy

> *Lord, I pray and declare that joy is our weapon. We choose joy now and ask You to come and clothe us in joy. Renew our minds. Set us afresh to keep pressing through with joy as our weapon against the assaults of the enemy. Jesus, we love You. Lord, I pray for the impartation of joy to be released over the reader right now. Amen.*

Now, allow yourself to feel joy! It's okay. Despite your circumstance, it's okay to feel supernatural joy! He bubbles in delight over you. Let His bubbling joy come over you right now.

Conclusion

Beloved warrior, you are not defeated! Having crossed through some trials and tribulations on this side of life, you carry experience and wisdom that cannot be matched by something you would learn from a textbook. Am I saying that God wants you to go through pain?

Absolutely not!

That's never the desire of a loving Father's heart. But I will say:

> *God causes all things to work together for good to those who love God, to those who are called according to His purpose* (Romans 8:28).

He is working something amazing and wonderful out of the tribulation you are going through, and you will see the other side of it. You may not be able to understand it right now, but God is there in the midst of it all.

> *Yet even in the midst of all these things, we triumph over them all, for God has made us to be more than conquerors, and his demonstrated love is our glorious victory over everything!* (Romans 8:37 TPT)

You were created to shine. You were created to be a carrier for His Presence. You were created to leak His glory. You were created to be free and not feel as a caged bird. You were created for destiny. You are to love and receive love wholeheartedly. You were created strong and mighty. You were created to not live in fear. You were created to trample on the schemes of the enemy and walk in victory. In the midst of any battle you may face, beloved, you are victorious! Simply put, *because of Him.*

Jesus' demonstration of His sacrificial love to us is what holds us up and gives us hope to face today. By His stripes you've been healed. By His stripes you are made whole. By His stripes you are restored. By His stripes you are set free from every assault or plan of the enemy. This is our inheritance. We are to walk as His warrior Bride. You are unstoppable as you match the heartbeat of the Father. Keep your focus on Jesus and worship Him despite any setback. May your faith be unwavering through any firing! Remember, "We are winning!"

I declare now over you: *"No weapon that is formed against you will prosper"* (Isa. 54:17). *"The Lord is a warrior; the Lord is His name"* (Exod. 15:3).

About the Author

Ana Werner and her husband, Sam, reside in Missouri with their two beautiful children. She is the founder of Eaglets Network and Ana Werner Ministries. Ana travels internationally and equips people to see in the Spirit, move in the prophetic, and experience healing and deliverance through her ministry. Her transparency as she shares the realities and experiences she has had in Heaven brings the Holy Spirit, the love of the Father, and the power of God into the room when she speaks. Ana is passionate about leading people into encountering Jesus' heart.

For more information visit: anawerner.org

Experience a personal revival!

Spirit-empowered content from today's top Christian authors delivered directly to your inbox.

Join today!
lovetoreadclub.com

Inspiring Articles
Powerful Video Teaching
Resources for Revival

Get all of this and so much more, e-mailed to you twice weekly!

LOVE TO READ CLUB
by DESTINY IMAGE